BLANKET STITCH
QUILTS

LYNNE EDWARDS

12 STUNNING PROJECTS FOR SIMPLE
STICK-AND-STITCH APPLIQUÉ

D&C
David and Charles

www.rucraft.co.uk

Contents

The Joys of Blanket Stitch

Until about ten years ago my experience of blanket stitch was very limited. Like so many other traditional sewing techniques, I acknowledged its existence and respected its role in the wider world of textiles but it wasn't for me, I thought. I did like the effect of outlining simple appliqué shapes with black hand-stitched blanket stitch, often seen on quilts from the 1930s and 40s, but why go to all that trouble needle-turning and stitching the edges of each appliqué shape on to a background, only to add more stitching over the top with the blanket stitching?

An alternative strategy would be to cut each piece of the appliqué design without any seam allowances and to stick it in place on the background fabric using an iron-on adhesive, also called a fusible web. Fusible web comes as a sheet of paper, smooth on one side and with a slightly rough texture on the other side, which is the glue in suspension. First, the appliqué shape is drawn on the smooth side of the fusible web and cut out roughly. It is then placed with the rough side down on to the wrong side of the chosen appliqué fabric and ironed, which sticks it firmly to the fabric. The design is then cut out exactly, cutting both the paper of the fusible web and the fabric at the same time. The paper backing is peeled from the cut shape of fabric before

flipping it over and positioning it right side upwards on the background fabric. A final pressing with the iron will bond the appliqué to the background, and it's ready for edging with blanket stitch. The appliqué will stay firmly in position, and the edges won't now fray. A brilliant solution, but still not for me.

The reason I remained unconverted to this method was because the layer of glue that fixes each piece of appliqué to the background takes away the softness of the fabric, making it feel stiff and inflexible, especially if the design has several layers of appliqué overlapping each other. As stroking fabric is one of my addictions, I just wasn't happy with this. Until the moment when I read in a book by the American machine quilter Debra Wagner her suggestion that as you only need to glue the edge of an appliqué shape to prevent fraying and to stick it to the background, why not only limit the fusible web to a narrow strip just around the edge of the fabric? This would take away any stiffness and still do the job. Of course, I thought – why didn't I think of that?

So, all credit to Debra and my heartfelt thanks. I started to design my first easy stick-and-stitch appliqué quilt immediately, and haven't stopped since. What I didn't know at the time was that I would find blanket stitching totally addictive, as do so many students that I have introduced to this technique. The extra bonus is that with the on-going sophistication of sewing machines, blanket stitch by machine has become so accessible. As I write this, my current handwork project is a large blanket stitch appliqué quilt, while I ring the changes with another smaller piece that is totally blanket stitched on my machine. How good is that?

All of the projects in this book can be blanket stitched by hand or by machine, and there are full instructions to help you to master both techniques. There are some lovely flower-inspired quilt designs, plus some fun motifs too, so look through, choose a design, and off you go!

Tools for the Task

Making a quilt of any description these days depends on a basic set of equipment – rotary cutting tools, general sewing equipment, probably a sewing machine, even if the essence of the technique to be used for the quilt is hand stitched. For the stick-and-stitch blanket stitch appliqué technique certain extras are needed and even fabric, threads and needles need consideration.

Cutting Equipment

Much of the cutting work with this technique is through the paper-backed fusible web, firstly on its own and then through paper and fabric that have been bonded together. A good pair of scissors is essential: I use a medium size pair, about 5½in (14cm) long with good-sized holes for my finger and thumb and sharp points. Tiny scissors will make the thumb joint ache very quickly, while a large pair is just too unwieldy for the precise cutting involved. I also have a very useful scissor-sharpener that I use regularly, so I'm not anxious about ruining my best scissors by cutting paper with them.

Fusible Web

There is a range of different fusible webs available, some more heavy duty than others and some with paper on both sides of the web to give more flexibility when handling the cut shapes. They all have their followers, so try out a few and find your own favourite. Avoid the heavy-duty versions though, as these will give too stiff an effect for the designs and projects in this book. My own favourite is Bondaweb, known in America as Wonder-Under and in Europe as Vliesofix, but even this brand needs treating with respect to avoid the film of glue from separating from the backing paper. I buy it as I

need it to avoid storing it for too long, and bring it home on a cardboard roll, never folded. Once home I cut it into page-size pieces and store them in a plastic folder away from radiators.

Fusible webs are a disaster if they get transferred by a hot iron to the base of the iron or the ironing board, spreading nasty black marks. I strongly recommend placing non-stick parchment baking paper, available from most supermarkets, on to the ironing board and another layer on top of the appliqué as you fuse the layers together to protect all the surfaces from the glue.

Appliqué Pressing Sheet

As well as fusible web, quilt shops often sell see-though non-stick appliqué pressing sheets, which although expensive are hugely helpful in assembling appliqué designs accurately and safely. The mat allows you to position all the various parts of an appliqué design, directly on to the non-stick surface rather than the fabric – see Essential Techniques: Using Fusible Web, step 5.

Fabric

With all quilts, the fabric chosen for it should be appropriate for the ultimate use of the project. A child's quilt will have to withstand rough treatment and frequent washing, whereas a wall hanging might only ever need a good shake and a freshen-up in the open air. For raw-edged blanket stitch work, choose medium-weight cotton fabrics if possible, as they work well with the fusible web and do not fray too much. Regular patchwork fabrics and batiks are ideal for this technique and make it very suitable to combine with other patchwork patterns in a project.

Hera

A hera is a plastic tool that is used mainly for creasing fabric. It has a pointed part that can be used to mark a temporary line or crease mark in fabric.

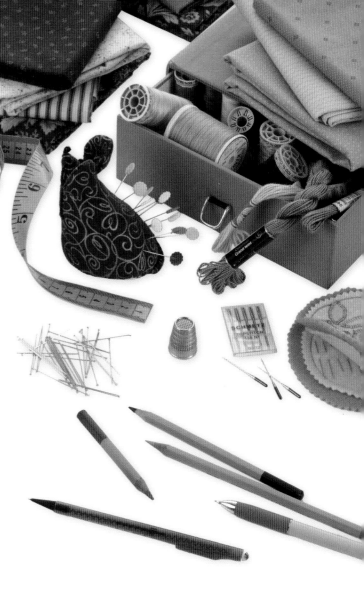

Threads

The thread used for blanket stitch appliqué can vary in thickness to reflect the design being stitched. A country-style quilt using homespun fabrics might look best outlined with a thicker thread, such as a cotton perlé or jean-stitch thread, as I used for the Pansy Baskets Quilt. If you are machine stitching the blanket stitch, test out the thicker thread as the top thread with a normal thread in the bobbin and adjust tension and needle size to suit.

Variegated and hand-dyed threads also look very effective and there are many lovely variegated machine threads that are perfect for this technique. Because the machine blanket stitch often uses a stitch sequence that doubles each stitch as it sews, a normal sewing thread looks much thicker and is as effective as a thicker thread used by hand.

My choice for hand blanket stitch on normal patchwork fabric is Gütermann silk thread, which is a little thicker than regular cotton sewing thread, but still fine enough to use on the closely woven fabric used in most quilts, especially batiks. Before embarking on the quilt itself, test the thread you are considering using on a sample to make sure it is compatible with the fabrics and will pull through the weave comfortably.

Needles

For hand blanket stitching with the Gütermann silk thread I like to use an appliqué needle (also called a Sharps) size 9 or 10 or the longer milliners needle (sometimes called a Straw) size 10. As the thread is a little thicker than regular sewing thread, I usually have to thread it with a needle threader, as both these needles have small eyes. With thicker thread, a crewel embroidery needle with its larger eye is most suitable, possibly a size 7 or 8. While a fine needle is best for the task as it will slip through the fabric layers easily, if you can't thread it or hold it comfortably, you may have to compromise and use a larger size.

For machine work using regular thread I use a machine needle 80/12, or a topstitch needle size 90 with variegated thread. Sometimes the machine companies have their own needles that they recommend, which is always a good guide, as they know what's best for their machines with the wide range of machine threads available these days.

Essential Techniques

This section describes the essential techniques you will need to create the blanket stitch appliqué for the projects in this book. More general techniques required for quilt making, such as adding borders, quilting and binding are described in General Techniques at the back of the book.

Stick-and-Stitch Technique

Each of the projects in this book features appliqué designs that are made using a stick-and-stitch technique, which is fully described here and can be referred to when any of the projects is being made.

Using the Design

Most of the appliqué patterns are printed full size as they appear in the quilt, although some will need to be enlarged. These patterns are used as a reference when arranging the separate pieces of fabric to build up the final appliqué design.

When using the stick-and-stitch technique, the appliqué shapes must first be reversed. The design is then separated into the various shapes that make up the final image. Any shape that is overlapped by another will need an extra amount added, about ⅛in (3mm) wide to the edge that will be overlapped. This is shown as a dashed line on the separate shapes and should be included when the shapes are traced on to the paper side of the fusible web. For each of the designs in the book, all the reversed pieces are shown labelled and grouped ready for tracing.

TIP

With this technique most of the inner section of the fusible is removed before the outline is ironed on to the fabric. If this inner area is large enough, I have placed one or more smaller outlines within it to be traced as positioned. Once that area of web has been cut and removed from the large drawn outline, the smaller shapes marked on it can then be cut out as usual.

Using Fusible Web

1 Place the fusible web smooth side *uppermost* over the reversed shapes of the design as given in each project. Trace each section including any dashed areas. Mark the grain line arrows and the numbers on the tracing, keeping these at the very edge of the shape rather than in the centre, as the centre area of fusible web will be removed later. The shapes can be traced closer together but leave about ½in (1.3cm) between each traced shape to make cutting out easier. Cut out each traced shape roughly ¼in (6mm) beyond the outer drawn line (see Photo 1 below).

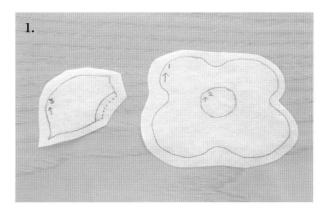

1.

2 Carefully cut out the central area of fusible web and remove it, leaving only about ⅛in (3mm) inside the drawn line (Photo 2). The removed pieces of fusible can be kept for later projects. If the removed area has extra, smaller shapes traced on to it, these can now be cut out in the same way (Photo 3 overleaf). Don't try to cut away the inner areas of any small or narrow pieces less than 1in (2.5cm) across as they are just too fiddly.

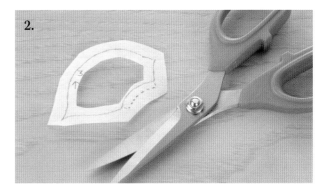

2.

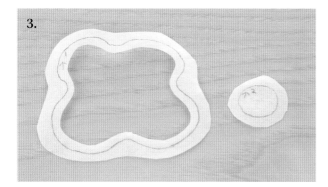

3.

3 Place each cut piece of fusible web rough side *downwards* on the *wrong* side of the fabric, matching the grain line arrow with the grain or weave of the fabric. Press with a hot iron to stick the web to the fabric.

4 Now cut accurately along the drawn line through both the paper and the fabric. Include in the cut-out shape any dashed area (Photo 4).

4.

5 The numbers on the reverse of each piece tell you the order in which to build up the design. If the design is very simple, it can be built up directly on the background fabric, using the drawing of the finished design as a guide for positioning each piece. Take the first piece, remove the paper backing and position the piece right side *up*, glue side *down* on the background. Add each fabric shape in turn until the design is complete. Dashed areas need to be overlapped by other pieces. When you are happy with the arrangement, press everything with a hot iron to fix the pieces in place.

For a more complex design where you need to be very accurate with the positioning of each fabric shape, use an appliqué pressing sheet or non-stick baking parchment paper to help. Lay the pressing sheet or paper over the drawn design – you will be able to see

the design through the plastic sheet. The non-stick baking parchment paper is less transparent, but should still allow the design to show through well enough for positioning the pieces on to it. The whole design is assembled piece by piece and ironed on to the pressing sheet or parchment paper (see Tip below). Once it is complete, only then will it be carefully peeled away from the background plastic or paper and re-positioned and ironed in place on the background fabric.

TIP

Fix the design and parchment paper or pressing sheet on to the ironing surface with pins or masking tape at the corners to keep everything in position as you stick.

Blanket Stitching by Hand

These guidelines for stitching the design by hand are for right-handed quilters. Left-handers need to study the photographs in a mirror to follow the step-by-step instructions. Start at the end of a piece of fabric, preferably where it is overlapped by another appliqué piece. Once you are more experienced, it can be your choice where you begin and finish, but this makes for an easier and less obvious starting point.

1 Turn the work so that the appliqué fabric is to the right and the background fabric is to the left. Keep the edge of the appliqué running straight towards you at all times at the point where you are stitching (see Photo 5).

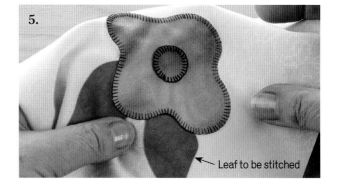

5.

← Leaf to be stitched

2 Make a knot at the end of the thread. Begin by bringing the needle up from the back in the background fabric close to the edge of the appliqué (Photo 6).

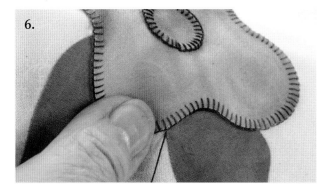

6.

3 Make one stitch at right angles to the edge of the appliqué and bring the needle back up in the same place as the thread (Photo 7). The needle should be horizontal when making this stitch. The stitch length is your choice. I like to make a stitch a generous ⅛in (3mm) with spacing between about half this. Don't worry too much – become comfortable with the stitching action and as you find a stitching rhythm your hand will settle into the spacing and size of stitch that it likes best.

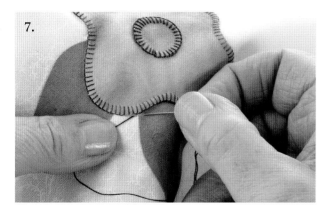

7.

4 Pull the thread across to the left to tighten the stitch, as shown in Photo 8.

8.

5 Hold the thread flat with your thumb (Photo 9). Bring the needle back to the appliqué, making a thread loop.

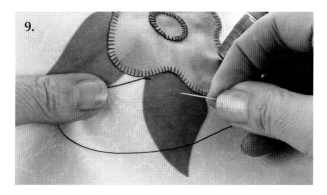

9.

6 With the edge of the appliqué running towards you, place the needle into the appliqué to match the end of the first stitch above it. Aim for a distance from the first stitch of about half the length of the first stitch. Keep the needle horizontal and at right angles to the appliqué edge and bring it out in the background fabric close to the appliqué (Photo 10).

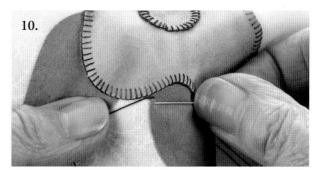

10.

7 Pull the thread to the left to tighten the stitch. The second stitch should be about the same length as the first stitch, at right angles to the appliqué edge (Photo 11).

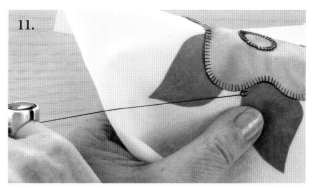

11.

8 Repeat steps 5–7 to make another similar stitch. This will be your pattern for making the stitches along the edge of the appliqué. As the design curves, turn the fabric in your hand so that the edge is always running straight towards you. This will create some curve and movement in the stitches, which will complement the curve in the appliqué design (Photo 12).

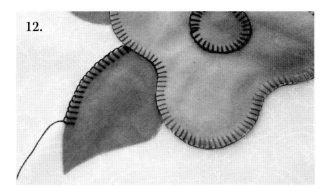

12.

9 To turn a sharp corner, following the principle of turning the fabric as you would on a sewing machine should result in an attractive mitred look in the corner stitches (Photo 13). To prevent the corner stitch from slipping to one side, leaving the fabric point vulnerable to fraying, make one extra tiny stitch on the spot at the corner to keep that long corner stitch in place (Photo 14).

13.

14.

10 To finish off, take the thread to the back of the work and make two or three tiny stitches in the background fabric, below the appliqué layer so that it's not visible on the front.

Blanket Stitching by Machine

For stitching a blanket stitch by machine, most instructions recommend using a clear plastic foot that is cut away at the front to give good visibility. I often stitch around an appliqué after the quilt has been layered with wadding (batting) and a backing fabric so that the blanket stitch acts as quilting though the layers. A walking foot is essential for this, preferably one that is cut away at the front like the plastic appliqué foot.

TIP

The walking foot is designed to move both top and bottom layers along at the same pace as it stitches. This has a stabilizing effect and I sometimes use this foot when blanket stitching around an appliqué on a single layer of background fabric as it can help to keep thinner fabrics from puckering as they are stitched.

Choosing the Stitch

Sewing machines are very sophisticated now and often have several variations of blanket stitch. As always, you need to get to know your machine thoroughly before you dive into a project. A piece of firm cotton fabric with a few pieces of plain fabric bonded on will allow you to experiment with each variation of stitch and to assess which one is best for your design. Use a normal cotton thread on the top and in the bobbin to start with so you can see just what each stitch does. Fabrics in solid colours are best so that every stitch can be clearly seen as you try them out. First, you need to assess the repeat pattern of stitches that is being made. Some machines have a whole range of variations of blanket stitch on offer but most will include one or more of the three shown in Figs 1a, 1b and 1c below.

If you have a computerized machine, you should be able to alter the width and the length of the chosen blanket stitch, which will fine-tune the dimensions of the stitch. Changing the stitch *width* will affect the length of the horizontal bar stitch that goes across the appliqué. Changing the stitch *length* will affect the length of the stitches that run along the edge of the appliqué, making the horizontal bar stitches closer together or further apart. Play with the settings and once you have decided on the best settings for the job, make a note of them directly on to the test fabric alongside the sample of stitching as a reference for later. I know we always think that we will remember, but, trust me, we don't…

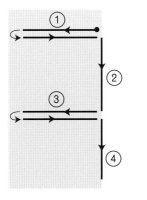

Fig 1a

In this version of blanket stitch the machine moves to the left horizontally across the appliqué and back to make a double stitch. Then it makes one single stitch alongside the edge of the appliqué before starting the sequence again by moving horizontally to the left across the appliqué as before. This stitch is the closest to hand blanket stitch.

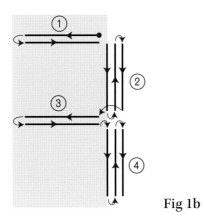

Fig 1b

In this version the machine moves to the left horizontally across the appliqué and back to make a double stitch. Then it makes a triple stitch by moving forward, back and then forward again along the side of the appliqué before starting the sequence again by moving horizontally to the left across the appliqué as before. This makes a stronger stitch line around the edge of the appliqué, which outlines it with more definition.

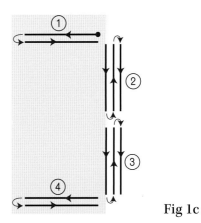

Fig 1c

Here, the machine moves to the left horizontally across the appliqué and back to make a double stitch. Then it makes a triple stitch by moving forward, back and forward again along the appliqué side. It repeats this triple stitch along the edge of the appliqué before starting the sequence again by moving horizontally to the left across the appliqué as before. This makes a firm outline of small stitches along the appliqué edge with two tiny stitches between each horizontal bar that goes across the appliqué itself. Sometimes it doubles the side horizontal movement to make four stitches on top of each other so all stitches are strongly emphasized.

Practising the Stitch

Once the stitch is selected, do some practice to get to know the rhythm of the machine's 'dance' pattern to make each stitch. If you have an up/down facility on your machine, use it here. If the 'needle down' setting is used when stitching, whenever the user stops the needle will automatically finish down in the fabric, so the work does not slip to the side – especially useful if you want to lift the pressure foot to adjust the direction of stitching slightly, as when stitching along the side of a curved appliqué edge.

Get comfortable stitching along straight edges and gentle curves first. For keeping snug to a curved edge, stop occasionally, raise the pressure foot and adjust the fabric so the appliqué edge is still running towards you. Try to stop and adjust the direction when the needle is stitching in background fabric. I have found I can control the machine to stitch just one stitch at a time when negotiating tricky areas by tapping the foot pedal once to make the machine do a single stitch and then finish down in the fabric again, which keeps me more in control.

TIP

A knee lift attachment is invaluable for slightly lifting the pressure foot so the direction of the fabric can be adjusted while still keeping hands and eyes on the work.

Turning Corners

You need to really study the stitching pattern of your machine for this, especially for sharp corners. Start with right-angled corners, which are not so difficult. To practise, take a double layer of firm fabric and draw a zigzag line on it, making it long with lots of zigzags with right-angled corners. Imagine that the line is the edge of an appliqué shape. This is quicker than actually bonding fabric samples to a background, as you will probably need to do this several times to improve your strategies. You could draw a series of shading lines where the appliqué fabric would be, as shown in Fig 2.

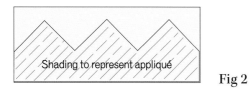

Shading to represent appliqué

Fig 2

Now, working slowly, blanket stitch along the line towards the first corner. Try to finish ready for a horizontal bar stitch at the exact corner with the needle sunk into the fabric – sometimes I tug on the fabric slightly to pull it back and squeeze the stitches together a little as I approach the corner to make the stitch finish right on the corner (Fig 3a). Lift the pressure foot slightly and swing the work round 45 degrees so that the next stitch, the horizontal bar stitch, will make a mitre at the corner. The direction you turn the fabric will depend on whether the corner is to the right or the left of the work (see Fig 3b and Fig 3c). Carefully stitch the bar stitch across and back again into the same spot at the corner, finishing with the needle down in the work. Lift the pressure foot slightly and rotate the work in the same direction as before until the drawn line to be stitched is running directly towards you as usual. Continue to stitch the entire line of zigzags, noting each time where the tricky areas are and trying to find your own strategies for achieving a good look. Once you are feeling reasonably comfortable with this, bond a square of contrast fabric on to a background fabric as a sample and blanket stitch around it to test your skills.

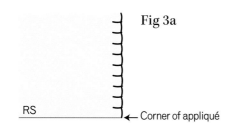

Fig 3a

RS ← Corner of appliqué

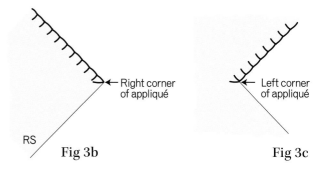

← Right corner of appliqué

RS   **Fig 3b**

← Left corner of appliqué

Fig 3c

Starting and Finishing

To machine blanket stitch around a square you need to start and finish inconspicuously without the join showing. Do not start at a corner but about ½in (1.3cm) from it (see Fig 4). Your machine may do several stitches on the spot to secure the thread before it begins its dance, but you will still need to take the threads to the back of the work after the stitching and knot them together for safety, so pull out at least 3in–4in (7.6cm–10.2cm) of both top and bobbin threads at the start to give you enough length to fasten off later.

Work your way around the shape and when you have turned the last corner and are approaching the starting point, slow down and try to manoeuvre the stitches so that they meet naturally. Leave long ends of both threads for tying off. If needed I undo the last couple of machine stitches if they look clumsy and use the same thread to stitch a linking stitch by hand to disguise the junction.

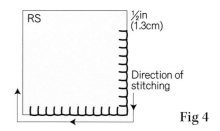

RS   ½in (1.3cm)

Direction of stitching

Fig 4

Stitching Sharp Points

For sharp outer points, follow the same strategies as described previously for right-angled corners but take it very slowly and when the point gets too narrow to allow two horizontal bar stitches to be made side by side, narrow the stitch width a little, stitch by stitch, as you approach the corner. Make a normal-width bar stitch at the corner itself and then reduce it again to stitch away from the corner. The bar stitches will overlap each other on either side but as long as they are all contained within the appliqué fabric this won't matter too much. Increase the stitch width once the appliqué is wide enough to accommodate it (Fig 5). Again, practise – draw leaf shapes on a doubled piece of firm fabric and stitch around them. Begin at the stem end of the leaf as that is the natural starting point, and stitch around it, adjusting at the leaf point with shorter bar stitches (Fig 6).

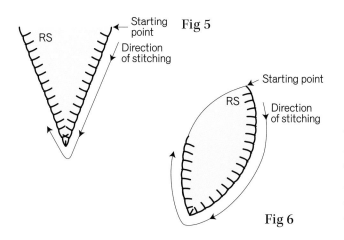

Making a Start

'All this practice – am I ever going to start?' I hear you cry? Sorry, but it takes a long time to unpick machine blanket stitch and it's better to make all the mistakes on scraps of fabric. I have highlighted the tricky areas rather than ignore them so you can recognize and sort them out at this early stage. Make sure your first projects have plenty of gentle outlines with not too many very sharp corners and you will surprise yourself with how quick and easy it is to achieve a stunning appliqué design.

Cutting Away the Layers

After stitching all the edges by hand or by machine, the layers may be reduced by turning the whole piece over and cutting away the background areas within the blanket-stitched edges ¼in (6mm) away from the stitching. This can make quilting easier but is not obligatory, so if you feel the extra layers add stability, then leave them intact.

This charming little cot quilt by Vicky Edwards uses fabric scraps in an irregular design of squares. She has blanket stitched by hand around some squares to highlight them and to appliqué a recycled piece of embroidery on to the quilt. The embroidery is slightly padded and framed with ribbon, giving the feeling of a Victorian crazy quilt.

Cherry Ripe

For some years I have used this traditional bunch of cherries appliqué block as the sample when teaching a day class on blanket stitch appliqué, usually by hand. The design is classic and very appealing, and its simplicity means that it doesn't take long to prepare and assemble one block and then it's straight into stitching around the edge. Lots learnt and achieved in one day – just what the eager student wants to happen in a one-off class.

When one of my regular students Pat Mitchell suffered a crisis of decision about her next quilt project, she felt she needed something that would provide plenty of quiet non-stressful stitching time with few design decisions to be made. She makes her quilts entirely by hand, and has a great love of rich reds, greens and gold, so we knew she would have plenty of fabrics in her stash ready to use in this design, plus a substantial length of cream calico that she just happened to have in her store. So the opportunity to make a dent in her collection of fabric was another reason to start tracing and cutting cherries straight away! I feel that the finished quilt is a real classic – colourful and striking. Pat called it 'Cherry Ripe' and announced with glee when she brought the finished quilt along to show the class that the only fabric she had bought for the project was the red fabric used for the binding on the edge of the quilt – everything else was from her stash. So now she feels justified in making a trip to a favourite quilt shop to fill up those spaces in the pile... don't we all?

The second project in this chapter is a simple cushion, which uses the cherry block from the quilt for the centre design. The cushion method I use here is simple and quick, without zips or piped edges, yet it still looks well-made and professional. As our son once said when small on being given a soft toy that I had made him, 'Did you really make this? But it's nearly as good as shop-bought'– praise indeed.

Cherry Quilt

This cherry design is stunningly simple but so effective, especially when repeated over the quilt with dramatic red sashing strips used to separate the blocks. The little windmills of green that make the cornerstones at the junctions of the red sashing strips give an extra touch of colour. Each block is made from a square of background fabric on to which the cherry design is appliquéd. When all the blocks have been stitched they are assembled with the sashing to make the quilt and the borders are then added.

There are thirty-five blocks in this quilt, arranged in seven rows, each row containing five blocks. More blocks could be added if you needed a larger quilt. You could alternate the cherry block with a nine-patch block, as Joan Webster did in her Daisy Quilt. Pat's arrangement here is the suggested size and layout but you could adapt the design to suit your own individual project. The cherries could be made from just one red fabric but it adds depth if several similar reds are used for both the cherries and the sashing strips. One green fabric was used for all the leaves in the appliqué design and for the cornerstone windmills and one brown fabric for the stems. There are five borders around the quilt, two wide borders using a green fabric with a large print and three narrow borders, one of red and two of the cream background fabric.

Requirements

- Background fabric 3½yd (3¼m)
- Assorted red fabrics for the cherries and sashing strips – 2yd/m in total
- Brown fabric for the stems ½yd/m
- Green fabric for the leaves and windmill cornerstones 2yd/m
- Red fabric for the narrow outer border ½yd/m
- Red fabric for the final binding ¾yd/m
- Green fabric for two wide outer borders 2½yd/m
- Wadding (batting) 81in x 103in (206cm x 262cm)
- Backing fabric 81in x 103in (206cm x 262cm)
- Fusible web 3yd/m (if using 17in/43.2cm wide type)
- Threads for the blanket stitch

Size of finished block:

9in x 9in (22.9cm x 22.9cm)

Size of finished quilt:

77½in x 99½in (197cm x 253cm)

TIP

Although this is a simple design, it is most effective if each block repeats exactly the position of the appliqué, so I would recommend using either a see-through appliqué pressing sheet or sheets of non-stick parchment baking paper when building up each cherry design (see Tools for the Task).

Making One Cherry Appliqué Block

1 Each cherry appliqué block needs a square of background fabric measuring 9½in x 9½in (24.1cm x 24.1cm). For this quilt you will need thirty-five pieces of background fabric of this size, one for each block. You may like to cut all the background squares at this stage ready to use, or cut each piece as you need it – your choice.

2 **Choosing the fabrics:** The cherry design can be seen full size in Fig 1 at the end of the project. Each block has three cherries, with two leaves and a bunch of brown stems. You may decide, like Pat, to mix the red fabric for the cherries for each block, varying them in each arrangement so that no two blocks are the same. Alternatively, you could place the colours in the same position for every block. Pat used one brown fabric for the stems and one green fabric for the leaves in each block, but you might like to use more fabrics in these shades through the quilt to give a more scrap look. The photograph here shows Pat's use of fabric in her blocks.

3 **Tracing the design:** When using fusible web the design must be reversed. Fig 2 (at the end of the project) gives each reversed shape to make the cherry design. The dotted lines should be included – they are the areas where one shape is overlapped by another. Place the fusible web smooth side *uppermost* over the six shapes in Fig 2. Follow the general instructions for tracing and cutting out the shapes from the fusible web in Essential Techniques: Using Fusible Web. Remove the inner section of fusible web from all the pieces except piece 1 (the stems), as they are very narrow and cutting away the inner areas is far too fiddly. Pieces 2 and 3 are the leaves; pieces 4, 5 and 6 are the cherries (see Fig 1).

4 Take the fabrics chosen for the design. Place each cut piece of fusible web with the rough side *downwards* on the *wrong* side of each chosen fabric, matching the grain line arrow with the grain or weave of the fabric. Follow the instructions in Using Fusible Web to iron the fusible web in place and to cut out each piece of the design.

5 **Building up the design:** Work on an ironing surface to position each piece, so at this stage trace the whole design from Fig 1 clearly on to thin paper or tracing paper. Alternatively, photocopy it to save time and energy. Cut a piece of non-stick parchment baking paper a little larger than the finished design in Fig 1 or use a see-through appliqué pressing sheet.

6 Place the paper or pressing sheet over your copy of Fig 1 on the ironing surface. Fix both layers in place with pins or masking tape at the corners. Starting with piece 1 (the stems), remove the paper backing. Position the piece right side *up,* glue side *down* in the correct place on the parchment paper or pressing sheet. Press lightly with the iron to stick it on to the parchment paper or pressing sheet. Alternatively, you can arrange the entire design and make any final adjustments before ironing anything. A final pressing of the whole piece will fix the design in place on the paper or pressing sheet.

7 Place piece 2 (a leaf) in position overlapping the end of the stem slightly and iron in place.

8 Similarly, arrange the other leaf (piece 3) in position, using Fig 1 beneath as a guide. Iron in place.

9 Repeat this process with the three cherries (pieces 4, 5 and 6) and press the whole design firmly with a hot iron to fix all the pieces on the background fabric.

10 **Stitching the design:** Pat stitched the design by hand, using a slightly thicker thread than usual, but if you wish to machine stitch it, that will be fine. She used Gütermann silk thread for her hand blanket stitch appliqué, using black thread throughout, which is the traditional colour used to outline appliqué, especially in the 1920s and 1930s. You could use several shades, matching the thread to the fabric, or perhaps a variegated thread. See the Threads and Needles section for more information. For information on stitching refer to Essential Techniques: Blanket Stitching by Hand and Blanket Stitching by Machine. I would stitch around the cherries first, then the stems and finish with the leaves, but you may prefer a different order of stitching – it is a personal choice rather than a specific strategy.

11 I often cut away the back layers after blanket stitching to reduce the thicknesses for quilting but on this occasion Pat chose to leave the background layers in place to give the design more stability.

Making the Rest of the Blocks

Making the first block always takes a long time: trying out stitches and threads, choosing fabrics, mastering the nuances of the design and so on. Once this block is completed, it becomes your reference for all those decisions made as you worked on it and making the others becomes far easier. If you are varying the fabrics from block to block, keep the finished blocks in view as you select the fabrics for the next cherry design as this will give an overview of the growing collection of blocks and ensure that the colours are evenly distributed in the quilt. If you look at the photograph of Pat Mitchell's quilt you will see the arrangement is seven rows of blocks, with five blocks in each row. Lay your blocks out in this arrangement as you make them so that you can check on the overall effect and balance of the fabrics used.

Sashing the Blocks

1 The thirty-five blocks are sashed with pieced cornerstones that give a windmill effect at the junctions of the sashing strips of the block (Fig 3). Arrange the thirty-five blocks in seven rows, each with five blocks.

Fig 3

2 From the group of red fabrics chosen for the sashing cut fifty-eight strips each measuring 2in x 9½in (5.1cm x 24.1cm). From the green fabric chosen for the cornerstones cut 124 squares each measuring 2in x 2in (5cm x 5cm).

CHERRY RIPE

3 To twenty of the cut sashing strips pin a square of cornerstone fabric at one end. Stitch diagonally across the square as in Fig 4. Note: the cornerstones must *always* be stitched in the same direction.

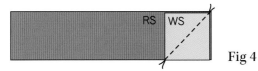

Fig 4

4 Trim both fabrics ¼in (6mm) beyond the stitched line (Fig 5). Press the cornerstone piece away from the strip, ironing from the front of the work (Fig 6).

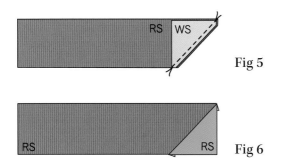

Fig 5

Fig 6

5 In the same way, pin and stitch a square of cornerstone fabric to *both* ends of the other thirty-eight sashing strips. Trim and press as before (Fig 7).

Fig 7

6 Pin and stitch four of the single-cornerstone sashing strips between the top row of blocks (Fig 8). Press the seams towards the sashing.

Fig 8

7 Repeat this for the bottom row of blocks but turn the sashing strips through 180 degrees to make the bottom row.

8 Pin and stitch three double-cornerstone sashing strips between the blocks of row 2 as in Fig 9. Repeat this arrangement with the blocks of rows 3, 4 and 5.

Fig 9

9 Join two single-cornerstone sashing strips and three double-cornerstone sashing strips in a long length together with four squares of cornerstone fabric as in Fig 10.

Fig 10

10 Make five more joined strips as in Fig 10. You should have four cut cornerstone squares of green fabric left over. Set these aside for later.

11 Pin and stitch the six long joined strips between the rows of blocks, matching the seams carefully (Fig 11). Press the seams towards the sashing. The quilt now should look like Fig 11, with the ends of all the red sashing strips around the outer edges of the quilt plain, without any green triangles of fabric on them.

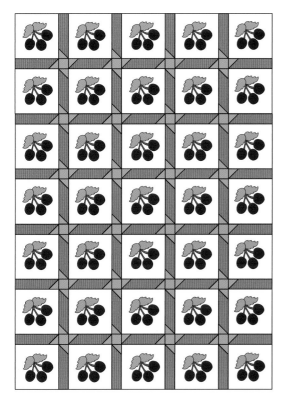

Fig 11

Framing the Quilt

12 Measure the quilt from top to bottom down the centre. From one of the red sashing fabrics cut two strips each 2in (5.1cm wide) in this measurement. Now measure the quilt from side to side and cut two strips of the same fabric each 2in (5.1cm) wide in this measurement. Take the two longer side strips and pin and stitch one to either side of the quilt. Press the seams outwards away from the quilt into the sashing.

TIP

If you don't have enough of one of your red fabrics to cut the long strips for this frame, don't worry. Just cut strips 9½in (24.1cm) long in the assorted red fabrics used for the sashing of the main quilt and join them together with cornerstone squares. The corner squares could be red like the sashing strips, or green. Seven strips and six cornerstones are needed for each side of the quilt (Fig 12a). Five strips and four cornerstones are needed for the top and bottom (Fig 12b).

Fig 12a

Fig 12b

TIP

If you look closely at Pat Mitchell's quilt, you will see that several of the sashing strips have a green triangle at the outer edge. They shouldn't be there but it really doesn't matter. What was an oversight on Pat's part is now part of a fine, original piece of work. Remember that when next you find, far too late, that there is an error in your piecing or stitching. If you can't put it right, just keep quiet and accept it, knowing that no one else will notice (or care)...

13 Take the two 2in (5.1cm) wide sashing strips cut earlier (or use the joined lengths shown in Fig 12b), and the four left-over cornerstone squares of green fabric (from step 10) and pin and stitch one at either end of each long strip (Fig 13). Press the seams towards the long strips.

RS

Fig 13

14 Pin and stitch one strip to the top of the quilt and the other to the bottom of the quilt, matching the cornerstone seams carefully. Press the seams outwards, away from the quilt.

Adding the Borders

There are a total of six border frames added to the quilt, which set the blocks in a pleasing surround and extend the size of the quilt in an effective way. Each time a border is added, the quilt is measured in both directions to make sure the border strips are cut to the right length to keep the quilt flat and to prevent it finishing up with wavy edges.

1 **First border (background fabric):** Measure the quilt from top to bottom. From the background cream fabric cut two strips each 1½in (3.8cm) wide and in a measurement to match the length of your quilt. Pin and stitch these to either side of the quilt. Press the seams outwards, away from the quilt.

2 Measure across the centre of the quilt from side to side. From the same fabric cut two strips 1½in (3.8cm) wide and in a length to match your own quilt measurement. Pin and stitch these strips to the top and bottom of the quilt. Press the seams outwards, away from the quilt.

3 **Second border (green fabric):** Measure down the centre of the quilt from top to bottom. Cut two strips from the chosen fabric 3½in (8.9cm) wide and a length to match your quilt length. Pin and stitch these to either side of the quilt. Press seams outwards as before.

4 Measure across the centre of the quilt from side to side. From the same border fabric cut two strips 3½in (8.9cm) wide and a length to match the width of the quilt. Pin and stitch these strips to the top and bottom of the quilt. Press the seams outwards.

5 **Third border (background fabric):** Repeat the process described in Adding the Borders, steps 3 and 4 with the cream background fabric, cutting the four strips 1½in (3.8cm) wide and in lengths to match the quilt. Press seams outwards from the quilt as before.

6 **Fourth border (red fabric):** Take the red fabric chosen for this border and repeat the process described in steps 3 and 4 above, cutting the strips 1½in (3.8cm) wide and in lengths to match the quilt measurements at this stage. Press seams outwards as usual.

7 **Fifth border (background fabric):** Measure the quilt as usual. Repeat step 5 above, with strips of cream background fabric cut 1½in (3.8cm) wide and in lengths to match the quilt.

8 **Final border (green fabric):** Repeat steps 3 and 4 above with the green border fabric, cutting the strips 5in (12.7cm) wide and in lengths to match the quilt. Press seams outwards.

Quilting and Finishing

Layer the quilt with wadding (batting) and backing fabric – see Quilting. Pat quilted her piece by hand, simply outlining the cherries and leaves in red thread and quilting close to the edges of the sashing strips in the same way. The cream borders were quilted close to the seams in red, leaving the other borders unquilted. Quilting is very personal – whether it's by hand or machine, minimal for the wadding requirements or densely quilted all over. As long as you are happy with the way you do it and the way it looks, that's all that matters. Finally, the edges were bound with red fabric to give a strong edge of colour to the quilt – see Binding a Quilt.

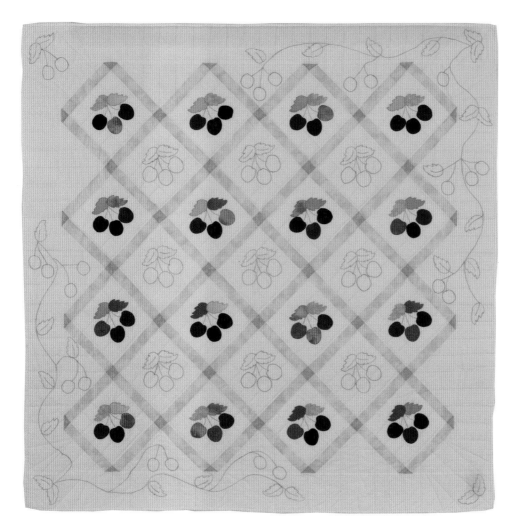

Marianne Bennett has given a very different feel to the cherry block by arranging the blocks on point in her quilt. She has alternated the blanket-stitched squares with hand-quilted blocks. The quilted lines have been given more strength by running a thread through each quilted stitch (called whipped stitch) – as shown in the diagram here.

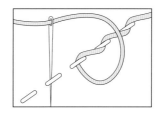

Patterns

Fig 1
Pattern – shown full size
Where the dashed blue lines cross indicates the
central point for placement of the appliqué motif on
the background square

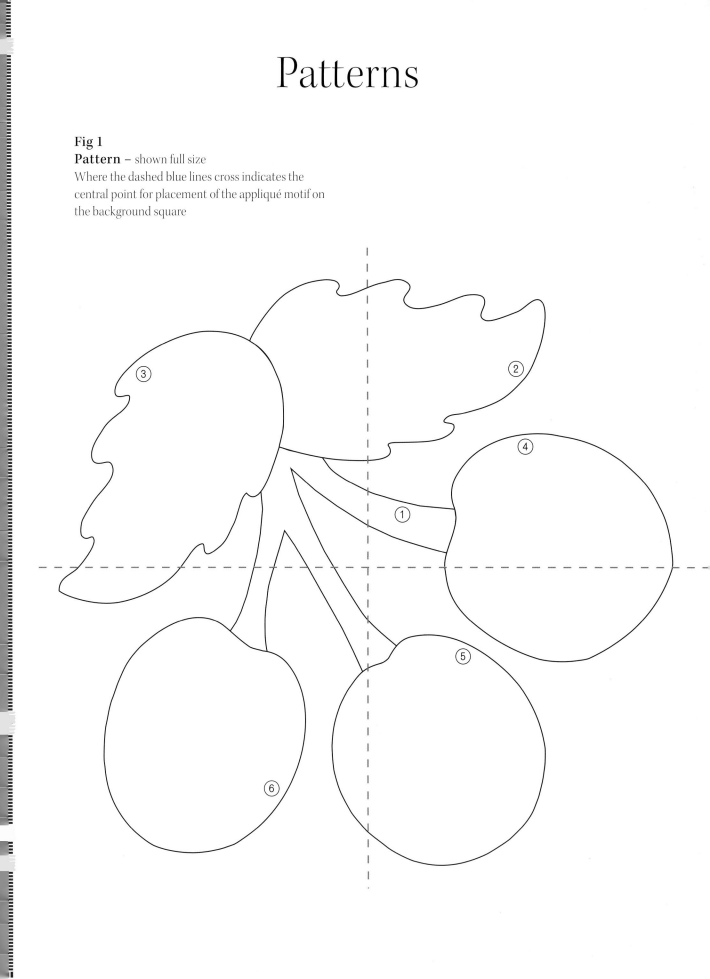

Fig 2
Pattern pieces (reversed) – shown full size
Dotted black lines indicate where one appliqué piece fits under
another and arrows indicate direction of fabric grain

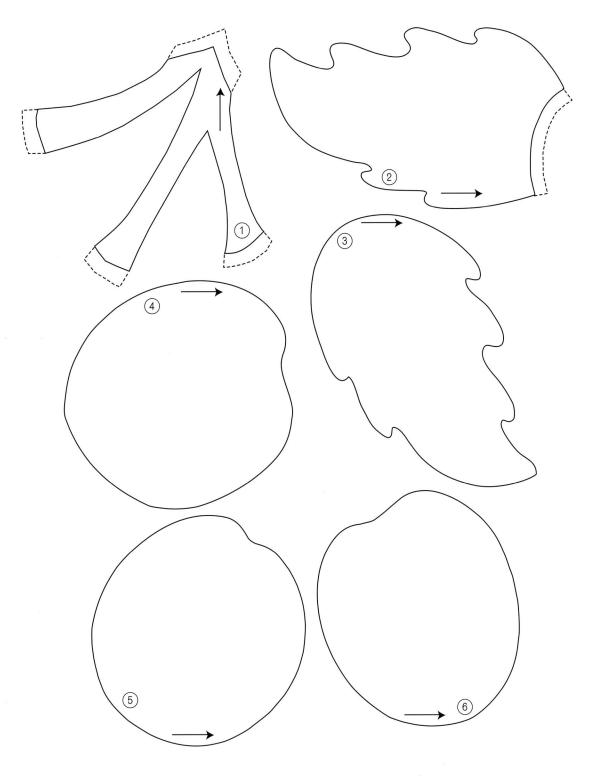

Cherry Cushion

The original design for these cherries dates back to those blanket-stitched quilts from the 1930s, so it seemed appropriate to use fabrics from a range of reproduction fabrics from that era, plus the traditional calico background. When I was collecting the fabrics for my Butterfly Quilt I took in every colour and print that I could find, as I was aiming for a really scrap quilt effect. I seldom use red in my quilts, but they were an essential part of the reproduction fabric range so I gritted my teeth and included several of them in my collection. All that agonizing, and then when it came to making the butterflies, the softer pastel shades seemed to work best together, so all my reds were set aside. However, their moment came with this cherry design: one fabric was used for the cherries and in the border squares, alternating with my favourite fabric of Scotty dogs and a third was used for the back of the cushion. I knew there was a good reason for buying them! The bonus with this cushion project is that the basic set of instructions can be adapted for different patchwork designs, with or without the centre panel. Use it for any future cushion projects to make a speedy and impressive gift or a wonderfully hand-crafted heirloom.

Requirements

- Background fabric for the centre block 9½in x 9½in (24.1cm x 24.1cm)

- Leaf fabric, all cut from a piece about 6in (15.2cm) square

- Red fabric (A) a fat eighth, for cherries and border squares

- Red fabric (B) a fat eighth, for border squares

- Fat quarter of fabric for cushion back

- Fat quarter of lining fabric for cushion back

- Fabric to line cushion front, lightweight calico (muslin) 16in (40.6cm) square

- Fusible web 8in (20.3cm) square

- Thin wadding (batting) 16in (40.6cm) square

- Threads for the blanket stitch

- Cushion pad 16in (40.6cm) square

Size of centre panel:

9in x 9in (22.9cm x 22.9cm)

Size of finished cushion:

15in x 15in (38.1cm x 38.1cm)

Making the Cherry Block

1 Cut a square of background fabric 9½in x 9½in (24.1cm x 24.1cm).

2 Using red fabric A and the green leaf fabric, follow steps 1–9 of the Cherry Quilt to cut and stick the cherry design on the background fabric. Use the cherry, stem and leaf patterns at the end of the quilt project. Stitch around the appliqué with blanket stitch, by hand or machine (see Essential Techniques: Blanket Stitching by Hand or Blanket Stitching by Machine).

Bordering the Centre Design

3 From each of the two red fabrics A and B cut eight squares, each 3½in x 3½in (8.9cm x 8.9cm). Take two squares of fabric A and one square of fabric B and pin and stitch together to make a strip (Fig 1). Press seams from the front towards fabric A. Repeat to make a second identical strip of three squares.

Fig 1

4 Take two squares of fabric A and three squares of fabric B. Pin and stitch these together in an alternating arrangement to make a strip (Fig 2). Press seams towards fabric A. Repeat make a second identical strip of five squares as Fig 2.

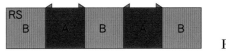

Fig 2

5 Pin and stitch a strip of three squares to either side of the centre block (Fig 3). Press the seams outwards, away from the centre block.

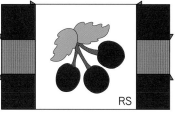

Fig 3

6 Now pin and stitch the two longer strips of five squares to the top and bottom of the block, matching the seams carefully (Fig 4). Press seams outwards, away from the centre block.

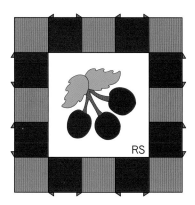

Fig 4

Layering the Cushion Front

7 Take the 16in (40.6cm) square of calico (muslin) and a similar cut square of thin wadding (batting). Arrange these with the wadding on top, matching the cut edges. Place the cushion right side up on top of the wadding and calico so that an equal amount of wadding shows all around the edge of the cushion top (Fig 5). Pin or tack (baste) the three layers together.

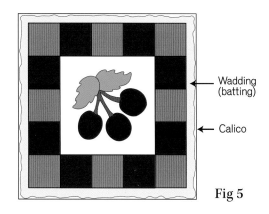

Wadding (batting)

Calico

Fig 5

Quilting the Cushion

I kept the quilting of the centre design very simple, just outlining the cherries and leaves by hand about $\frac{1}{8}$in (3mm) away from the edges of the appliqué in a slightly thicker thread in the same calico shade. I also quilted a simple frame about 1in (2.5cm) from the edge of the centre background square. I then enjoyed myself hand stitching a decorative border around the block. Using the same thread as before, I first stitched two parallel lines of quilting in a big stitch, as in Fig 6a, which shows the actual size of the stitching. I then used the same thread and stitched spaced cross stitches, stitching through the top layer into the wadding but not through to the back of the work (Fig 6b).

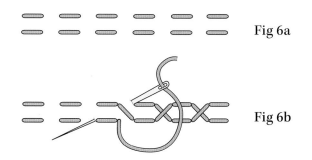

Fig 6a

Fig 6b

Completing the Cushion

8 The back for the cushion is made from two overlapping pieces, which I like to line with a toning fabric to give the cushion back more substance. From the fabric chosen for the back of the cushion (I used a red Thirties print) cut two pieces, each 16in x 10$\frac{1}{2}$in (40.6cm x 26.7cm). Cut two pieces of lining fabric to this same measurement.

9 Take one piece of back fabric and one of lining fabric, place these together with right sides facing and matching edges exactly. Pin and stitch them together along one of the long sides (Fig 7a). Repeat this with the other pair of back fabric and lining.

10 Press seams open. Flip the lining fabric over so the two fabrics are wrong sides facing. Press along the stitched seam and pin or tack (baste) the two layers together, matching fabric edges exactly (Fig 7b).

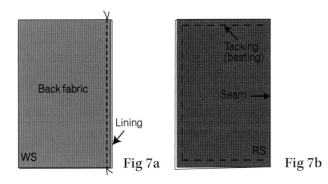

Fig 7a

Fig 7b

TIP

Pressing the seam open at this stage will encourage the fabrics to fold cleanly at the stitched edge when the lining is flipped to the back of the main fabric.

11 With the cushion back fabric upwards, machine a topstitch ¼in (6mm) from the seamed edge (Fig 8a). Machine another topstitched line 1in (2.5cm) from the seamed edge to give a firm finish to the backing piece (Fig 8b).

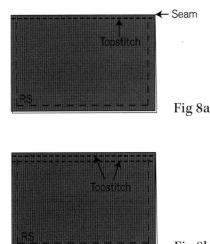

Fig 8a

Fig 8b

12 Repeat steps 10 and 11 with the second pair of back fabric and lining pieces.

13 Trim the quilted cushion front to 15½in x 15½in (39.4cm x 39.4cm).

TIP

If your quilted cushion front is less than 15½in (39.4cm) square, don't panic. Just trim the three layers to match the top layer, making sure the top measures the same on all sides. If it's half an inch smaller it won't matter – you will just have a slightly smaller cushion.

14 Trim the two cushion back pieces along one of the short sides so that the longer side measures 15½in (39.4cm) (or measurement to match the size of your trimmed cushion top) (Fig 9). The width of each back piece should be about 10¼in (26cm).

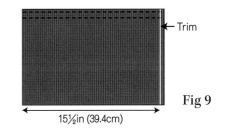

Fig 9

15½in (39.4cm)

15 Place the cushion front right side *up* on a flat surface. Arrange the two back pieces right side *down* with their raw edges matching the edges of the cushion front and the folded edges overlapping across the centre (Fig 10).

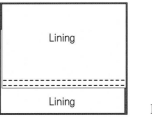

Fig 10

16 Pin the front and back together and machine stitch all around the outer edges with a ¼in (6mm) seam. Trim the corners a little to reduce bulk.

17 Turn the cushion through to its right side and press the outer seam. Machine stitch a line about ½in (1.3cm) from the edge all around the cushion – this gives it an extra finish around the outer edges.

Art Deco Rose

I first used this design way back when I devised the Second Sampler Quilt course for my regular students to tackle. It was a rose design based on an Art Deco stencil, which I thought would be perfect for a block using reverse appliqué. When we try a new technique, sometimes we discover that it just doesn't suit our hands or our hearts. While full of admiration for those who like a challenge, we are far more likely to complete a project if we are loving making it. Making a sampler quilt gives an opportunity to try one block only of many techniques and at the end of it we have a wonderful, complex quilt and we also know just which techniques are going to be our favourites in the future.

Over the years though I found that while quilters loved the look of this rose design, they often struggled with the reverse appliqué technique, as it calls for very precise needle-turning and stitching. Meanwhile I had discovered the joys of blanket stitch appliqué and was already using this design as a sample in my teaching, so I decided to drop the tricky reverse appliqué block in the sampler quilt and replace it with the totally addictive blanket stitch technique. My reasoning seems to have worked, because the first time I included it, Judy Baker-Rogers promised herself that once she had finished her sampler quilt she would make a quilt for her daughter using just this one block design. Her own sampler quilt was included in the revised combined edition, published in 2010 as *The Essential Sampler Quilt Book*, and here she is again with the promised quilt, now used continuously on her daughter's bed for the past three years. What greater compliment could we quilters ask for?

Art Deco Rose Quilt

As with many complex appliqué designs, the rose block looks most effective when used alternately with another, simpler block. The pictures here show how Judy Baker-Rogers used a square of background fabric quilted in the same rose design with contrasting thread, to great effect. She also edged each block with a narrow border of dark blue/purple before the sashing strips, which frames each block beautifully. The final wide border to the quilt is enhanced with a smaller version of the centre of the block design, again an appliquéd rose alternating with a quilted rose. Altogether a quilt to die for I feel.

The design consists of a central rose motif with surrounding leaves placed on an inner circle of contrasting fabric, with a decorative ring of appliquéd shapes running around it at a distance. All these are arranged on a square of background fabric. This means one fabric for the rose petals, one fabric for the six leaves, a third fabric for the inner background circle and a fourth for the outer ring of shapes. The outer ring could be made from one of the first three fabrics if you prefer to limit the fabrics used. The background fabric is used for the appliqué blocks, for the alternating quilted squares in the quilt and also for the final wide border.

Requirements

- Background fabric for all blocks and final wide border, 5yd (4½m)
- Four fabrics used in appliqué blocks and rose designs in the final border, ¾yd/m of each
- Fabric for narrow framing strip around each block plus quilt binding, 2yd/m
- Fabric for sashing between the blocks, 1½yd/m
- Wadding (batting) 93in (236cm) square
- Backing fabric 93in (236cm) square
- Fusible web 4½yd/m (if using 17in/43.2cm wide type)
- Threads for blanket stitch

Size of finished block:

12½in x 12½in (31.8cm x 31.8cm)

Size of finished quilt:

91in x 91in (231cm x 231cm)

TIP

Appliqué designs can often be adapted and used as quilting patterns, as Judy did here. Three different shades of thread were used to give the design more clarity and interest.

Making an Appliqué Rose Block

1 Each appliqué rose block needs a cut piece of background fabric 13in x 13in (33cm x 33cm). For this quilt you will need thirteen pieces of background fabric this size, one for each appliqué block, plus twelve pieces of background fabric also cut 13in x 13in (33cm x 33cm) to be used for the alternating quilted blocks. You may like to cut all the background squares at this stage ready to use, or cut each piece as you need it.

2 **Transferring the design to fabric:** Use the patterns at the end of the project instructions (enlarged as described there). To make a master copy of the rose design, trace the *whole* design on to paper, using the two parts of Fig 2, matching up the dashed lines and referring to Fig 1 if necessary. Fold the square of background fabric lightly into four. Use the fold lines as a guide for positioning the appliqué design – the dashed lines on the master copy should match the fold lines on the background fabric. Mark the appliqué pattern on the *right* side of the background fabric square by tracing the design, using a sharp marking pencil and light box if necessary. The traced lines are a guide for positioning the cut pieces of appliqué fabric, so trace lightly just *inside* the drawn line so that these lines will be hidden when the appliqué shapes are placed over them. If the fabric is too dark for the design to be traced through, use dressmaker's carbon paper and a tracing wheel. (I use an empty, fine ballpoint pen to mark the design through the carbon paper.)

TIP

If your background fabric is light in colour and the master copy is made with a strong drawn line you might not have to trace the outlines on to the background fabric. Instead, after preparing and cutting out all the pieces of the design ready for assembly on the background, place the master copy on the ironing board and pin the background fabric right side *up* over it on the board. If you can see the shapes on the master copy clearly through the fabric, use these as a guide for positioning each piece of appliqué and ironing it in place.

3 **Tracing the pieces:** When using fusible web, the design must be reversed. Fig 3a (at the end of the chapter) shows the centre part of the design reversed ready to be traced with fusible web. Fig 3b below shows the shape for the outer ring reversed ready for fusible web. Trace the shapes in Fig 3a on to the smooth side of the web. Mark the numbers and grain line arrows on the tracing, keeping these at the very edge of each shape, as the centre part of the web will be removed later. Trace the shape in Fig 3b on to the smooth side of the web twelve times, marking the grain line arrow on each as before.

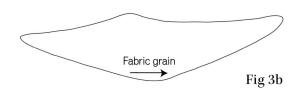

Fabric grain

Fig 3b

4 From the traced design, cut out the centre rose pattern in one piece (which includes the numbered shapes 1–7), roughly just beyond the drawn lines to separate it from the rest of the design (Fig 4a). Now carefully cut about ⅛in (3mm) *inside* the drawn lines of shapes 4, 5, 6 and 7 (Fig 4b). Do not attempt to cut away inside pieces 1, 2 and 3 as they are just too small and fiddly.

Fig 1

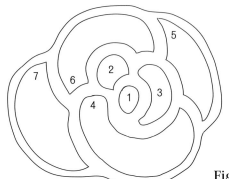

Fig 4a

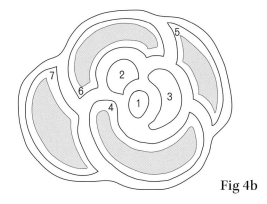

Fig 4b

care that each piece covers the drawn outline on the square of background fabric, using the centre part of Fig 1 as a guide. When you are happy with the arrangement, press everything with a hot iron to fix the pieces in place.

5 Place this piece of fusible web rough side *down* on the *wrong* side of the fabric chosen for the rose, matching the grain line arrow on piece 3 with the grain or weave of the fabric. Follow the instructions in Essential Techniques: Using Fusible Web, to iron the fusible web in place and to cut out each piece of the design to make the seven segments of the rose.

6 From the traced design, cut out roughly each of the six leaves, (numbered 8–13), cutting just beyond the drawn lines. Carefully cut away the fusible web about ⅛in (3mm) *inside* each leaf as before.

7 Place each leaf shape of fusible web rough side *down* on to the *wrong* side of the chosen fabric, matching the grain line arrows with the grain or weave of the fabric. Iron the fusible web in place and cut out each piece of the design to make the six leaves.

8 Repeat this process with the six segments (numbered 14–19) that make the inner background circle, ironing them to the *wrong* side of the fabric chosen for this part of the design. Do not cut away the fusible web inside pieces 15 and 17 as they are too small.

9 Repeat the process to make the twelve pieces needed for the outer ring of the design.

10 **Building up the design:** Remove the backing paper from each of the pieces. Begin with the centre of the design, leaving the outer ring of shapes until later. Arrange the pieces of the rose, the leaves and the inner background circle segments in position on the background fabric, right side *up*, glue side *down*, taking

11 Now arrange the twelve cut pieces that make the outer ring in position in the same way, matching each piece of fabric with the drawn outline on the background square and making sure that each piece fully covers the drawn line each time. Press with a hot iron to fix the pieces in place.

12 **Stitching the design:** Judy stitched her design by hand using Gütermann silk thread in colours to match the appliqué fabrics, but if you wish to machine stitch that will be fine. See Tools for the Task: Threads and Needles for more information. For blanket stitching refer to Essential Techniques: Blanket Stitching by Hand or Blanket Stitching by Machine. Stitching order is a personal choice but I suggest you start by stitching around the larger shapes, like the leaves, before moving on to the smaller petals of the rose.

13 I often cut away the back layers after blanket stitching to reduce the thicknesses for quilting, but for this design where the pieces do not overlap each other, the appliqué fabrics are stabilized by leaving all the layers intact.

14 Once you are happy with your first appliqué rose block, continue to make a total of thirteen blocks in the same way.

Making a Quilted Rose block

15 If you have not yet cut the squares of background fabric for the quilted blocks, cut all twelve squares now, each 13in x 13in (33cm x 33cm). All the squares need to be marked for quilting at this stage I'm afraid – just when you are longing to get the whole thing together and see how it looks! You could leave the quilt-marking until the quilt top is assembled but tracing the design on to separate squares is so much easier.

16 Use a light box to trace the rose design from your master copy (see previous step 2) on to the *front* of a cut square of background fabric, using a suitable marking pencil. I use a watercolour pencil in a shade similar to the fabric but slightly darker. This wears off in time and washes out. Mark each of the twelve blocks for quilting in the same way.

Framing the Blocks

17 Check that each block measures 13in x 13in (33cm x 33cm) at this stage. From the fabric chosen for the narrow frames, cut two strips measuring 1in x 13in (2.5cm x 33cm) and two strips 1in x 14in (2.5cm x 35.6cm) for each block – a total of fifty strips in each length for all twenty-five blocks.

18 Pin and stitch a shorter strip of framing fabric to either side of each block (Fig 5a). Press the strips outwards, away from the block, ironing from the front.

19 Pin and stitch a longer strip of framing fabric to the top and the bottom of the blocks (Fig 5b). Press the strips outwards, away from the block as before. Each block should now measure 14in x 14in (35.6cm x 35.6cm).

Fig 5a

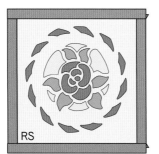

Fig 5b

Assembling the Quilt

1 **Sashing the blocks:** All sashing strips are cut 2¼in (5.7cm) wide. From the chosen sashing fabric cut twenty strips each 2¼in x 14in (5.7cm x 35.6cm).

2 Arrange the twenty-five framed blocks in five rows each of five blocks.

3 Pin and stitch four sashing strips between the top row of blocks (Fig 6). Press the seams towards the sashing strips. Repeat this for each of the remaining four rows of blocks.

Fig 6

4 Measure across each row of joined blocks – they should all be 75in (190.5cm). From the sashing fabric cut four strips each 2¼in x 75in (5.7cm x 190.1cm). Pin and stitch the strips between the five rows of blocks as Fig 7. Press seams towards the sashing strips.

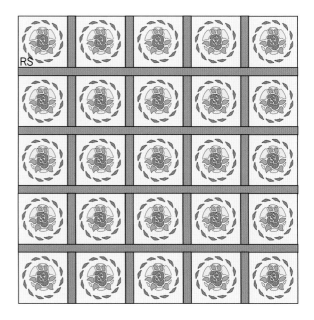

Fig 7

TIP

If your rows of blocks do not measure 75in (190.5cm), don't worry. Press with steam to get all the rows measuring the same as each other and cut the long horizontal strips to match this measurement.

5 Measure the quilt from top to bottom down the centre. Cut two strips of sashing 2¼in (6.4cm) wide in this measurement. Pin and stitch one to either side of the quilt. Press seams outwards away from the quilt.

6 Measure the quilt from side to side across its centre. Cut two strips of sashing 2¼in (6.4cm) wide in this measurement. Pin and stitch one strip to the top of the quilt and the other to the bottom. Press the seams outwards away from the quilt as before.

7 **Adding the final border:** Measure the quilt down the centre as before. From the border fabric cut two strips each 6½in (16.5cm) wide and in a length to match the quilt – you will probably have to join two strips of fabric together. Measure across the quilt from side to side and cut two strips 6½in (16.5cm) wide and in a length to match this second measurement. Ideally these four long strips should all be the same measurement, but if they are not, follow the actual measurements of your quilt and cut the strips to match. Finally, cut four squares of border fabric for the cornerstones each 6½in x 6½in (16.5cm x 16.5cm).

8 At this stage it is best to trace the smaller rose design shown in the Fig 8 pattern on to the border strips and cornerstone squares so that they can be blanket stitched before attaching the strips to the main quilt. Each long strip has five appliqué rose designs on it with four quilting designs alternating with the appliquéd versions. To mark the positions for the appliqué designs, first find the centre of the border strip by folding it in half. Mark along one long edge from the centre fold with a marking pencil every 15¼in (38.8cm) in both directions (Fig 9a) – a total of four marks plus the centre fold. Fold the strip at each marked point as in Fig 9b.

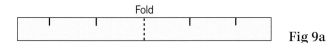

Fold

Fig 9a

Fig 9b

TIP

Lay the marked strip on to a row of blocks in the quilt. Ideally the folded lines on the strip should roughly match the centre of each block. If they do not, adjust the folded lines to match your quilt blocks. Do this with each of the four border strips.

9 Make a master copy of the small rose design by tracing it from the Fig 8 pattern on to paper. Follow the technique used previously (step 2, Transferring the Design to the Fabric) to mark each border fabric strip with five rose designs, positioning each rose by matching the dashed line on the master copy with the folded lines on the strip.

10 Fig 10 (pattern given at end of chapter) shows the rose design reversed for tracing on to fusible web. Use the same process as before (steps 3–10 of Making an Appliqué Rose Block) to trace, cut and stick each piece in position to assemble the rose designs on all four border strips.

11 Repeat the process to assemble the rose design also on to each of the four cornerstone squares of border fabric.

12 Blanket stitch each appliqué block by hand or machine in the same way as the main blocks.

13 Find the mid-points between each appliqué block on the border strips by folding, as before. Use the fold lines to position the master copy as previously and trace the design on to the fabric ready for quilting.

14 **Adding the final border:** The quilt is now edged with a narrow framing strip of fabric to match the frames that were added to each block earlier. Cut two strips of framing fabric each 1in (2.5cm) wide and in a length to match the side border strips. Pin and stitch a strip to either side of the quilt. Press seams outwards.

15 Pin and stitch a long appliquéd border strip to each side of the quilt. Press the seams into the narrow framing strips. Measure the quilt from side to side across the centre. Cut two strips of framing fabric 1in wide and a length to match this measurement. Pin and stitch them to the top and bottom of the quilt. Press seams outwards.

16 Cut four strips of the narrow framing fabric, each 1in x 6½in (2.5cm x 16.5cm). Pin and stitch one to either end of the two remaining appliqué border strips (Fig 11a). Press seams towards the framing strips.

17 Pin and stitch a cornerstone square to either end of each long appliqué border strip (Fig 11b). Press the seams into the narrow framing strips.

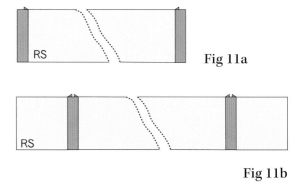

Fig 11a

Fig 11b

18 Pin and stitch these long borders to the top and bottom of the quilt, matching the narrow framing strips exactly.

19 **Quilting the design:** Layer the quilt with wadding (batting) and backing fabric – see Quilting. Judy quilted all of her quilt by hand. She outlined the rose appliqué pieces by stitching in the narrow channels between the pieces, and also quilted in the seams of the narrow framing strips to emphasize them (known as quilting in the ditch). The quilting of the rose design outlines in the alternating blocks was done with thicker thread and larger stitches to give the blocks real impact, even at a distance.

20 Finally, the quilt was bound in the same framing fabric, echoing the narrow strips used in the quilt – see Binding a Quilt.

Patterns

Fig 2
Pattern (top half) – shown reduced,
so enlarge by 166% on a photocopier
Match up the dashed lines on both
templates to create the whole pattern
Arrows indicate fabric grain

Fig 2
Pattern (bottom half) – shown reduced, so
enlarge by 166% on a photocopier

Fig 3a
Pattern for Centre (reversed)– shown
reduced, so enlarge by 166% on a photocopier

Fig 8
Border Rose Pattern – shown
reduced, so enlarge by 166% on a
photocopier

Fig 10
Border Rose Pattern (reversed design)– shown reduced, so enlarge by 166% on a photocopier

Pigs in Clover

I live in a village in Suffolk in England where pigs have always been part of the landscape. These endearing animals have such character and lend themselves so well to appliqué quilts, either for children or for the many people around who just love pigs. My first piggy wall hanging was a special gift for my dear friend Wendy Crease, who is a pig addict. I later adapted the design to make this baby's cot quilt, which could also be displayed as a wall hanging. I incorporated banks of clover as half-size blocks so that the piggy blocks could be staggered in the design to give a more interesting arrangement. This quilt was made with great success by one of my regular students Dorothy Pickford. Her friend Denie Reed noted how intricate the banks of clover were and quietly decided to simplify the design to make the little quilt shown at the end of the project. When I asked her who this quilt was for, she stated firmly, 'Me'. And why not?

The pig design is used again as an appliqué motif on a peg bag, described after the quilt project. It pleases me to see the revival of interest in old-fashioned household objects like tea-cosies, aprons and peg bags. They are seen as fashionably retro and slightly ironic in today's high-tech world, but still lovely for whatever the reason. One of my regular students used to churn out peg bags by the dozen for years as a fund-raiser, and now suddenly finds them hugely in demand again. I took the opportunity to wheedle the pattern from her and adapt it to make this jolly piggy peg bag. Other appliqué designs, such as the smaller Art Deco rose or the butterfly used in the table runner, could easily be used for the appliqué on the peg bag instead of the pig design in future projects if preferred.

Pigs in Clover Cot Quilt

There are two pigs used in this quilt design, one facing to the front and the other sideways. I also reversed the side-facing pig pattern to give a third variation in the collection of pigs. Each pig is placed on a square of background fabric and all the blanket stitching is completed before the blocks are joined together to make the quilt top. I used three fabrics for the background squares: I had intended using just two, but found, as ever, that I didn't have enough to make all nine blocks from these fabrics, so added one square of a third fabric for the background of the centre block. Running out of fabric is always good as the introduction of more fabrics makes the quilt richer, I feel – at least, that's what I tell myself. When I quilted the piece I found that my ace sewing machine has a decorative stitch that looks like a four-leafed clover, so I used that as part of the quilting to complement the pigs in clover theme.

Requirements

- Three fabrics for background squares: four 10in (25.4cm) squares from two of the fabrics and one 10in (25.4cm) square from the other fabric

- Pigs: a fat quarter of textured pink fabric for the body and snout and a fat quarter of plain pink fabric for the head and feet

- Eyes: black fabric 6in (15.2cm) square

- Clover leaves: fat quarter of dark green fabric

- Sashing fabric and background fabric for the clover leaf blocks ½yd/m

- Border fabric ½yd/m

- Wadding (batting) 45in x 40in (114cm x 102cm)

- Backing fabric 45in x 40in (114cm x 102cm)

- Binding fabric, two strips 2½in x 41in (6.4cm x 104cm) and two strips 2½in x 46in (6.4cm x 117cm)

- Fusible web 1yd/m (if using 17in/43.2cm wide type)

- Threads for blanket stitch and decorative machine stitching

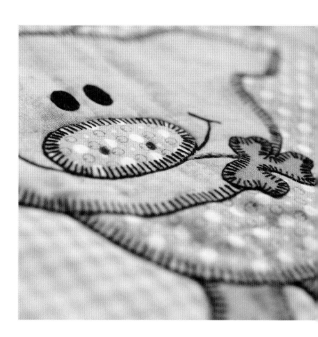

Size of finished block:

9½in x 9½in (24.1cm x 24.1cm)

Size of finished quilt:

39½in x 37¼in (100.3cm x 94.6cm)

TIP

Because the pigs are arranged by eye on each square of background fabric, I would recommend using either a see-through appliqué pressing sheet or sheets of non-stick parchment baking paper when building up each pig. Once completed, they can be removed from the paper or pressing sheet and placed as desired on the background fabric (see Tools for the Task: Fusible Web).

Design Decisions

1 There are two pig appliqué designs, one front-facing and one side-facing. More variations can be made by reversing the side view pattern so that the pig is facing the other way. Nine pigs are needed in total, so spend a little time deciding which of the two designs is going to be used on each of the background fabrics.

Making the Front-Facing Pig

2 **Tracing the design:** Use the patterns given at the end of the project instructions, enlarging them as described there. The front-facing pig is given in Fig 1. When using fusible web the design must be reversed. Fig 2 gives each reversed shape to make the front-facing pig. Include the dashed lines. Place the fusible web smooth side *uppermost* over the ten shapes in Fig 2. Follow the instructions given in Essential Techniques: Using Fusible Web, for tracing and cutting out the shapes from the fusible web. Remove the inner section of fusible web from piece 5 (the body) and piece 6 (the head). When the inner area is cut from piece 5, the smaller pieces 1, 2, 3, 4, 7, 8, 9 and 10, which are drawn in this area, will now be ready to cut out in the same way. Remove the inner part of piece 7 (the snout) but not the other pieces as they are too small and fiddly.

3 Take your two pig fabrics. Place each cut piece of fusible web with the rough side *down* on the *wrong* side of each chosen fabric, matching the grain line arrow with the fabric grain. Pieces 8 and 9 are used for the eyes, while piece 10 is the clover leaf. Iron these on the *wrong* side of the appropriate fabrics. Follow the instructions in Essential Techniques: Using Fusible Web to iron the web in place and to cut out each piece.

4 **Building up the design:** Work on an ironing surface to position each piece. Trace the whole design from Fig 1 on to thin paper or tracing paper or photocopy it. Cut a piece of non-stick parchment baking paper a little larger than the finished design in Fig 1 or use a see-through appliqué pressing sheet.

5 Place the paper or pressing sheet over your copy of Fig 1 on the ironing surface. Fix both layers in place with pins or masking tape at the corners. Starting with feet pieces 1, 2, 3 and 4, remove the paper backing. Position the feet right side *up*, glue side *down*

in the correct place on the parchment paper or pressing sheet. Press lightly with the iron to stick them on to the paper or sheet. Alternatively, arrange the entire design and make any final adjustments before ironing anything. A final pressing will fix the whole design in place.

6 Now place piece 5 (the pig's body) into position and iron it in place. Arrange piece 6 (the head) on the body and iron that into place. You could place the head in position by eye, rather than exactly following Fig 1 – that way each pig will be slightly different and individual.

7 Remove Fig 1 from the ironing board and use it as a guide to position the eyes, snout and clover leaf on the pig. Again, a little variation with each pig will add character.

8 Gently peel the completed design from the paper or pressing sheet. Position the completed pig in the centre of the background square of fabric. Press with a hot iron to fix the design in place.

9 Trace from Fig 1 or draw freehand the pig's smile, tail and the stem of the clover on to the design.

10 Repeat this process with all the front-facing pigs on their chosen background fabric. I made five front-facing pigs for my quilt.

Making the Side-Facing Pig

11 Fig 3 given at the end of the project instructions shows the side-facing pig. Fig 4 shows the reverse pattern for the fusible web for the side-facing pig. Follow the same process as before for tracing and cutting the fusible web. Begin with the feet when positioning the design (pieces 1–4) and finish with the clover leaf (piece 10). Press with a hot iron to fix the pieces in position.

12 Repeat this process with all the side-facing pigs. I used three pigs facing this way and one pig facing in the opposite direction. To reverse the direction the pig is facing, trace Fig 4 and flip the tracing over before using it as a pattern for the fusible web.

13 **Stitching the design:** I stitched around each pig and the clover leaves in the pigs' mouths in blanket stitch by hand, using Gütermann silk thread in the traditional black throughout, but whether you stitch by hand or machine is your choice. For blanket stitching refer to Essential Techniques: Blanket Stitching by Hand or Blanket Stitching by Machine. See also Tools for the Task: Threads and Needles for more information on your choices. Before stitching around the eyes, snout and clover leaf, the layers of the appliqué may be reduced by turning the whole piece over and cutting away the background area within the blanket-stitched edges ¼in (6mm) away from the stitching. This is not obligatory, so if your nerve fails you, just leave the layers intact. I like to cut away the back layers to make quilting easier and to give the quilt more life. Use embroidery thread to stitch the stem of the clover leaf and the pig's smile and tail, either in backstitch or stem stitch. Use French knots to stitch the nostrils on the snout.

Making the Clover Blocks

There are three blocks of clover, roughly half the height of the piggy blocks but the same width. These are placed with the three rows of pigs to offset the arrangement and give it an informal look – pigs don't usually line up in rows, after all… The chosen sashing fabric is used for the background fabric in these three blocks. Fig 5 shows the positions of the clover half-blocks with the large square pig blocks.

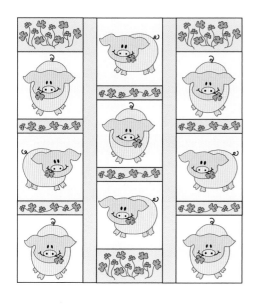

Fig 5

14 Cut three pieces of sashing fabric each measuring 5¼in x 10in (13.3cm x 25.4cm).

15 Using Fig 6, trace the large leaf (A) twice on to the smooth side of fusible web. Trace the other large leaf (B) four times and the small leaf five times on to the fusible web. This will give the eleven leaves needed for one block of clover. I find it easier to complete each clover block before starting on the next.

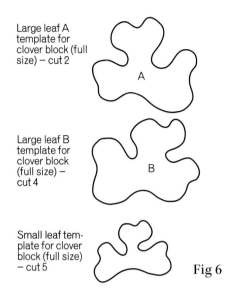

Large leaf A template for clover block (full size) – cut 2

Large leaf B template for clover block (full size) – cut 4

Small leaf template for clover block (full size) – cut 5

Fig 6

16 Cut out the leaves from the fusible web roughly ¼in (6mm) beyond the drawn line. Don't try to cut away the web inside the leaves as they are too small.

17 Place each cut piece of fusible web rough side *downwards* on the wrong side of the clover fabric. Press with a hot iron to stick the fusible web to the fabric. Now cut accurately along the drawn lines through both paper and fabric – you should have six large leaves and five small leaves.

18 Use a light box to trace just the clover stems, *not* the leaves, from the design in Fig 7 on to the front of each piece of fabric.

19 Remove the paper backing from each leaf. Arrange the eleven leaves on the stems with right sides *up*, glue side *down*, using Fig 7 as a guide. Iron the leaves on to the fabric to stick them down.

20 Repeat steps 15–19 twice more to make the three clover blocks needed for the quilt.

21 Stitch around each leaf using blanket stitch. Stitch the stems of the leaves with embroidery thread, using either backstitch or stem stitch.

Making the Clover Leaf Sashing

22 Cut six strips of sashing fabric, each measuring 2in x 10in (5.1cm x 25.4cm).

23 Trace the small clover leaf and the large clover leaf B from Fig 8 three times each on to the smooth side of fusible web – this will give the six leaves for one sashing strip. Complete the design on one strip before starting on the next. Follow steps 16 and 17 above to make the six leaves for one sashing strip.

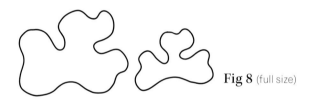

Fig 8 (full size)

24 Use a light box to trace just the clover stems (not the leaves) from the design in Fig 9 on to the front of each strip of sashing fabric.

25 Remove the paper backing from each leaf. Arrange the six leaves on the stems with right sides *up*, glue side *down*, using Fig 9 as a guide for positioning before finally ironing on to the fabric to stick them down. Stitch around each leaf and the stems as you did before.

26 Make the remaining five sashing designs of clover leaves in the same way.

Assembling the Quilt

1 Arrange the completed nine pig squares and clover areas as shown in the main photograph.

2 Pin and stitch the left-hand vertical row (Fig 10). Press the seams towards the clover areas, ironing from the front of the work.

3 Pin and stitch together the middle vertical row of blocks (Fig 11). Press seams towards the clover areas.

4 Pin and stitch the right-hand vertical row, ironing as before. Measure each row of blocks from top to bottom. At this stage all three should measure 36¾in (93.3cm). If they do not, adjust the seams.

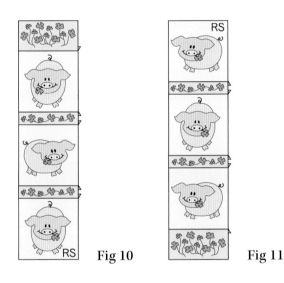

Fig 10   Fig 11

5 Cut two long strips of the fabric used for the clover sashing each 2in x 36¾in (5.1cm x 93.3cm). Place them between the three vertical rows of blocks as Fig 12.

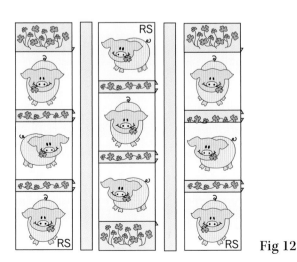

Fig 12

6 Pin and stitch the rows of blocks to the vertical sashing. Press the seams towards the sashing strips, ironing from the front of the work (Fig 13).

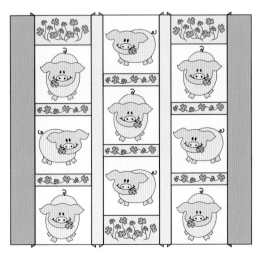

Fig 13

7 Adding the borders: For the border cut two strips each 4in x 36¾in (10.2cm x 93.3cm). Pin and stitch a strip to either side of the quilt. Press the seams outwards, away from the quilt (Fig 14).

Fig 14

8 Cut two strips of the same fabric, each 4in x 39in (10.2cm x 99.1cm). Pin and stitch to the top and bottom of the quilt. Press seams outwards (Fig 15).

Quilting and Finishing

9 Layer the quilt with wadding (batting) and backing fabric – see Quilting. Pin or tack (baste) the layers together ready for quilting either by hand or machine. I quilted by machine around the pigs close to the blanket stitching and around the snout, leaving the rest of the pigs unquilted to keep them puffy. I also quilted in the seam around each block to give definition. I used a decorative stitch on my machine to quilt ¼in (6mm) from the long edges on both vertical sashing strips and added more surface quilting in the wide border. Either hand or machine quilting is fine, or a combination of both.

10 Finally, bind the quilt in a dark green fabric to blend with the outer border – see Binding a Quilt.

Denie Reed simplified the Pigs in Clover design for this charming little quilt, alternating a nine-patch block with the appliqué blocks to give an Irish Chain look to the quilt.

Fig 15

Patterns

Fig 1
Pattern for Front-Facing Pig – shown reduced, so enlarge by 133% on a photocopier

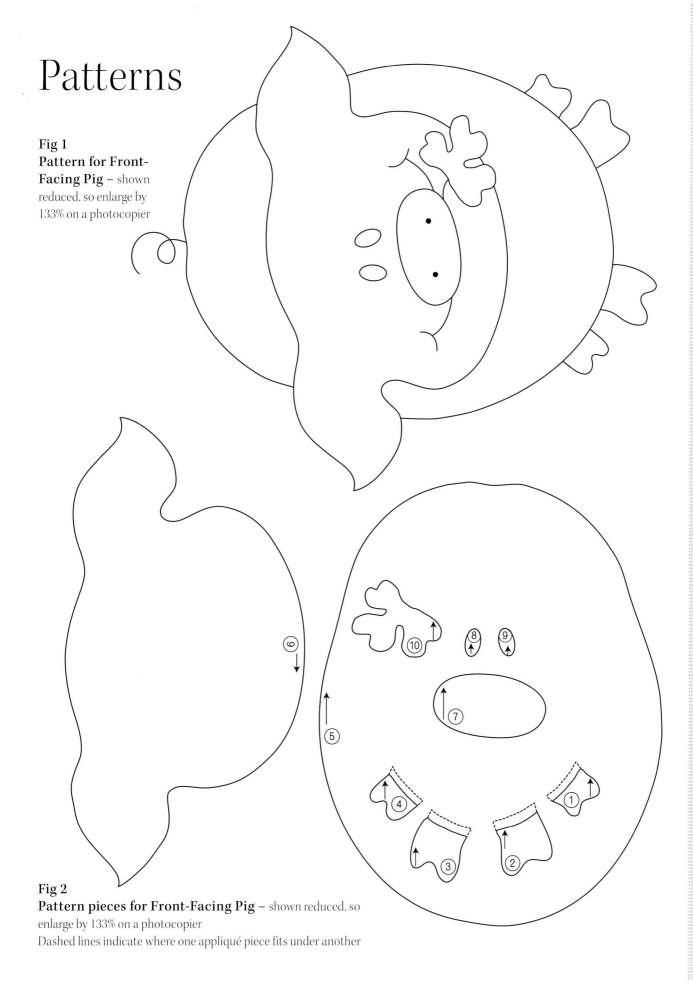

Fig 2
Pattern pieces for Front-Facing Pig – shown reduced, so enlarge by 133% on a photocopier
Dashed lines indicate where one appliqué piece fits under another

Fig 3
Pattern for Side-Facing Pig – shown reduced, so enlarge by 133% on a photocopier

Fig 4
Pattern pieces for Side-Facing Pig – shown
reduced, so enlarge by 133% on a photocopier

Fig 7
Pattern for Clover Design – shown reduced, so enlarge
by 133% on a photocopier
Rectangular shape indicates size of background fabric

Fig 9
Pattern for Clover Scroll – shown
reduced, so enlarge by 133%
Rectangular shape indicates size of
background fabric

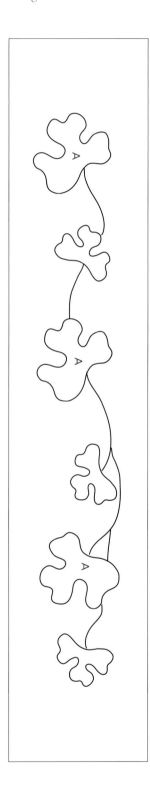

Piggy Peg Bag

The pig on this peg bag is a smaller version of the one used in the Pigs in Clover Cot Quilt, although any simple motif could be adapted for blanket stitch appliqué and used for the front of the bag – try other designs from the book. It could also be a useful way of using up left-over 2½in (6.3cm) wide jelly roll strips, which could be joined together horizontally and then used as the main bag fabric.

The original pattern was very much based on dress-making skills, with the seam allowances much wider than the ¼in (6mm) that we quilters are used to. I have adapted it to make it easy for us to stitch and hopefully have made the step-by-step instructions more detailed than the usual dress pattern versions, which tend to assume a background knowledge in the reader far beyond my own experiences... There is also a small bit of basic carpentry involving a short length of dowelling (a wooden pole with a circular cross-section) and a cup-hook but very easy – even I had no trouble with it. The bag is lined with a contrast fabric, which I also used as part of the pig appliqué.

Requirements

- Main bag fabric ½yd/m
- Lining fabric, also used for part of the pig appliqué, ½yd/m
- Fabric for the pig appliqué 6in–8in (15.2cm–20.3cm) square
- Extra scraps of fabric for the flower, eyes and butterfly
- Piece of dowelling ⅝in (1.5cm) diameter x 3¼in (8.3cm) in length
- Cup-hook
- Fusible web about 11in x 9in (28cm x 22.9cm)
- Threads for blanket stitch

Size of finished bag:

16¾in x 10¼in (42.6cm x 26cm)

TIP

Because the pig is arranged by eye on the front of the bag, I would recommend using either a see-through appliqué pressing sheet or sheets of non-stick parchment baking paper when building up the pig. Once completed, it can be removed from the paper or pressing sheet and placed as desired on the front bag fabric (see Tools for the Task: Fusible Web).

Constructing the Bag

1 **Making the bag pattern:** Use the patterns given at the end of the project instructions, enlarging them as described there. The front and back pattern pieces for the bag are identical and together create the shape in Fig 1. The lower section of the pattern is shown in Fig 2a and the upper section in Fig 2b. Figs 2a and 2b are half of the shape needed and must be traced and joined together to make the complete pattern, as follows. Cut a piece of tracing paper (or greaseproof paper or freezer paper) 9in x 12in (22.9cm x 30.5cm). Fold the paper in half lengthwise to measure 9in x 6in (22.9cm x 15.2cm) (Fig 3a). Trace the lower section from Fig 2a on to the paper as in Fig 3b, placing the folded edge of the paper on the dashed line marked 'fold' on the lower template pattern. Trace the grain line arrow from the pattern.

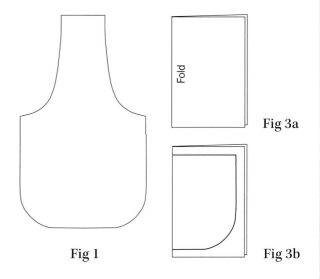

Fig 1

Fold

Fig 3a

Fig 3b

2 Hold the tracing paper firmly and cut through both layers along the drawn lines, leaving the folded edge uncut (Fig 4a). Unfold the paper to make the complete lower section of the bag shape (Fig 4b).

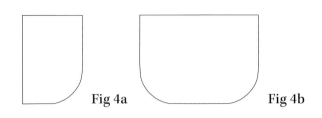

Fig 4a   Fig 4b

3 In the same way, take a piece of tracing paper 11in x 12in (28cm x 30.5cm). Fold it in half lengthwise so it measures 11in x 6in (28cm x 15.2cm). Trace the top section of the pattern from Fig 2b, placing the folded edge of the paper on to the dashed line as before. Cut out the shape and unfold it (Fig 4c).

4 Join the two pattern pieces together edge to edge without overlapping (Fig 4d).

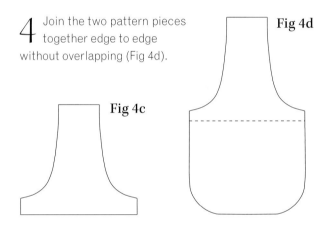

Fig 4d

Fig 4c

5 **Cutting the pieces:** Fold the main bag fabric in half, matching the selvedges and press. It doesn't matter whether it is folded right sides facing or wrong sides. Pin the paper pattern to the fabric, matching the fabric weave with the arrow on the pattern and pinning through all layers to keep everything in place (Fig 5).

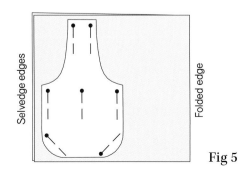

Selvedge edges   Folded edge

Fig 5

TIP

Fabric is woven more tightly and is less likely to stretch along the weave that runs parallel to the woven selvedge edge. Whereas the weave that runs across the fabric from selvedge to selvedge is stretchier. Your bag will keep its shape far better if the pattern is placed parallel to the selvedge edges as in Fig 5, with the tight weave running from the top to the bottom of the bag.

6 Cut around the edge of the pattern using scissors to keep the outline as accurate as possible.

7 Repeat this process with the lining fabric. You will now have two pieces of bag fabric and two identical pieces of lining fabric.

Adding the Appliqué

8 The appliqué pig in Fig 6 is much the same as the Pigs in Clover Cot Quilt, the only difference being that it is a little smaller and the clover leaf has been replaced with a flower and a butterfly added to the background area. For the peg bag project I did not remove the centre area of fusible web from any of the pieces, apart from the pig's body and head, as they are all too small.

9 When using a fusible web, the design must be reversed. Fig 7 gives each reversed shape to make the pig and also the free-flying butterfly. The dashed lines should be included – they are the areas where one shape is overlapped by another. Place the fusible web smooth side *uppermost* over the eleven shapes in Fig 7. Follow the instructions given in Essential Techniques: Using Fusible Web for tracing and cutting out the required shapes from the fusible web. Remove the inner section of fusible web from piece 5 (the body) and piece 6 (the head). When the inner area is cut from piece 5, the smaller pieces 1, 2, 3 and 4 which are drawn in this area will now be ready to cut out in the same way. Similarly, when the inner area of the head is cut out, pieces 7, 8, 9 and 10 will be ready to cut out. Remove the inner part of piece 7 (the snout) and the flower and butterfly if you wish to, but not the other pieces as they are just too small and fiddly.

10 Take the two fabrics chosen for the pig. Place each cut piece of fusible web with the rough side *downwards* on the *wrong* side of each chosen fabric, matching the grain line arrow with the grain or weave of the fabric. Pieces 8 and 9 are used for the eyes and piece 10 is the flower. Iron these on the wrong of the fabrics chosen for these. Follow the instructions given in Essential Techniques: Using Fusible Web to iron the fusible web in place and to cut out each piece.

11 **Building up the design:** Work on an ironing surface to position each piece. Trace the whole pig design from Fig 6 clearly on to thin paper or tracing paper (or photocopy it). Cut a piece of non-stick parchment paper a little larger than the finished design in Fig 6 or use a see-through appliqué pressing sheet.

12 Place the paper or pressing sheet over your copy of Fig 6 on the ironing surface. Fix both layers in place on the ironing surface with pins or masking tape at the corners. Starting with pieces 1, 2, 3 and 4 (the feet), remove the paper backing. Position the feet right side *up*, glue side *down* in the correct place on the parchment paper or pressing sheet. Press lightly with the iron to stick them on to the parchment paper or pressing sheet. Alternatively, arrange the entire design and make any final adjustments before ironing anything. A final pressing of the whole piece will fix the design in place.

13 Place piece 5 (the pig's body) into position and iron it in place. Arrange piece 6 (the head) on the body before ironing that into place. Remove Fig 6 from the ironing board and use it as a guide to position the eyes, snout and flower on the pig.

14 Gently peel the completed design from the paper or pressing sheet. Trace from Fig 6 or draw freehand the pig's smile, tail and the flower stem on to the design.

15 Position the pig and butterfly on the right side of one of the cut pieces of bag fabric, using the photograph of the project to help with positioning. Press with a hot iron to fix the appliqué in place.

16 **Stitching the designs:** I stitched around all the appliqué shapes by hand using a pink Sulky cotton thread in a thicker quality (a 12 thickness rather than the usual 8). Whether you stitch by hand or machine is your choice, of course. For stitching either by hand or machine, refer to Essential Techniques: Blanket Stitching by Hand or Blanket Stitching by Machine. See Tools for the Task: Threads and Needles for more information.

17 Use embroidery thread to stitch the stem of the flower and the pig's smile and tail, either in backstitch or stem stitch. I was able to use the same Sulky thread as the thickness was just right for the hand embroidery.

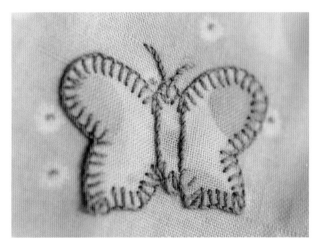

Making Up the Bag

1 Place the two pieces of bag fabric right sides facing and pin together along the bottom curved side, matching the curved edges carefully. Stitch the usual ¼in (6mm) seam, reversing the stitching for about ¼in (6mm) at either end to secure the seams (Fig 8). Turn the bag right side out and press along the seam lightly, making sure as you do so that the seam is right at the edge on the bag.

Fig 8

TIP

To reduce the bulk of the seam allowance I trimmed the edges with pinking shears after stitching to within ⅛in (3mm) of the stitched line. If you do not have pinking shears, clip the curved seam allowances using a small pair of scissors with sharp points, snipping at roughly ¼in (6mm) intervals, and keeping ⅛in (3mm) away from the seam itself (Fig 9).

Fig 9

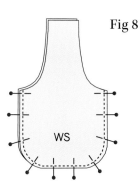

2 Repeat step 1 above to stitch together and trim the two lining shapes. This time do not turn the lining right side out. Instead, press lightly along the stitched seam on the wrong side.

3 Measure and press over to the wrong side a ½in (1.3cm) turning at each of the two narrow ends of the bag lining. Pin these in position (Fig 10).

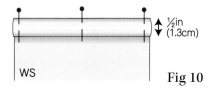

½in (1.3cm)

WS

Fig 10

4 Drop the bag with its right sides outwards into the lining. This means that both bag and lining will be right sides facing. Match the side seams and curved edges exactly. Pin the curved edges along one side ready for stitching (Fig 11).

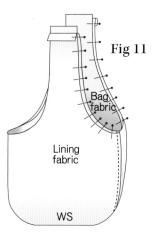

Fig 11

Bag fabric

Lining fabric

WS

5 Starting at the top edge of the bag fabric begin stitching along the pinned edges with the usual ¼in (6mm) seam, stitching through the folded-back edge of the lining and right around the curved edges, finishing by stitching through the folded lining at the other end of the seam and right to the end of the bag fabric. Trim the curved seam allowance with pinking shears as before or clip the curves. In the same way, pin and stitch the other long curved seam on the bag. Trim the seam allowance with pinking shears or clip the curves.

6 Remove the pins from the turnings in the lining. Gently pull the bag fabric through one narrow open end until the whole bag is pulled through and is right side outwards, with the lining in its correct place. Both bag and lining will now be stitched together with wrong sides facing and the only raw edges are at the two narrow ends of what will be the bag handle. Press the stitched seams lightly, making sure as you do so that all the seams are right at the edge on the bag.

7 **Joining the handle:** Turn the bag with the lining side outwards to get at the two open ends more easily. Measure across one of the handles, along the folded edge of the lining fabric. It should measure 3¼in (8.3cm). Mark the centre point on the wrong side of the bag fabric, ½in (1.3cm) down from the top raw edge of the handle (Fig 12a). Also mark ¼in (6mm) on either side of the centre (marked A and B in Fig 12b).

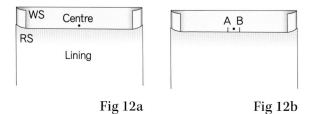

WS   Centre

RS

Lining

Fig 12a

A B

Fig 12b

8 Pin the two raw edges of both bag handles together, matching the top edges and side seams exactly. Do not pin the folded edges of the lining fabric – just the main bag fabric (Fig 13a). Stitch a ½in (1.3cm) seam through the pinned layers of the bag fabric only (not the lining fabric) from one outer end to mark A. Reinforce each end of the seam by reversing the stitching at the start and at mark A. Repeat this from the other end of the pinned handles, stitching to mark B and reversing at either end of the seam to reinforce it (Fig 13b). This gives a top seam joining the handles together with a ½in (1.3cm) gap at the centre.

Fig 13a   **Fig 13b**

9 Finger-press the seam allowances open, including across the centre gap. Tuck the seam allowances under the two folded edges of the lining fabric as neatly as possible. Pull the folded edges of the lining fabric so they meet and pin in position (Fig 14a). Stitch the folded edges together by hand, leaving the centre ½in (1.3cm) unstitched to match the gap in the main bag fabric (Fig 14b).

11 Place the bag on a flat surface and mark a line with a fabric marker or hera 1¼in (3.2cm) from the top seam on the handle. Stitch along the line through all layers, reversing at either end to reinforce it (Fig 15).

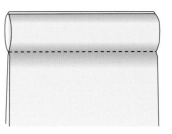

Fig 15

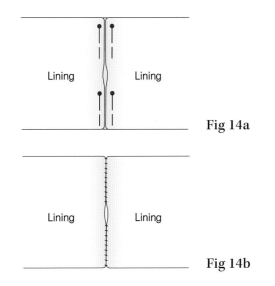

Lining   Lining

Fig 14a

Lining   Lining

Fig 14b

12 Cut a piece of ⅝in (1.5cm) diameter dowelling 3¼in (8.3cm) long. Mark the centre with a pencil 1⅝in (4.1cm) from either end of the dowelling. Screw a cup-hook into the wood at the pencil mark. Do this by pushing firmly and turning the hook round and round – it should soon embed itself into the wood. Once the hook is screwed far enough into the dowelling to be secure, remove it by turning in the opposite direction (remember the useful saying 'righty-tighty, lefty-loosey').

10 Topstitch by machine along both long seams at the top of the bag – I used a decorative stitch on my sewing machine to add interest.

13 Slide the dowelling into the top of the bag handle, above the line of stitches just stitched. Align the screw-hole in the dowelling with the gap in the stitching at the top of the bag handle. Securely screw the hook back into the dowelling through the gap in the top seam, using the original hole in the wood. So now you can do household carpentry as well as making quilts... Your piggy peg bag is now complete – hang it up and use it!

Patterns

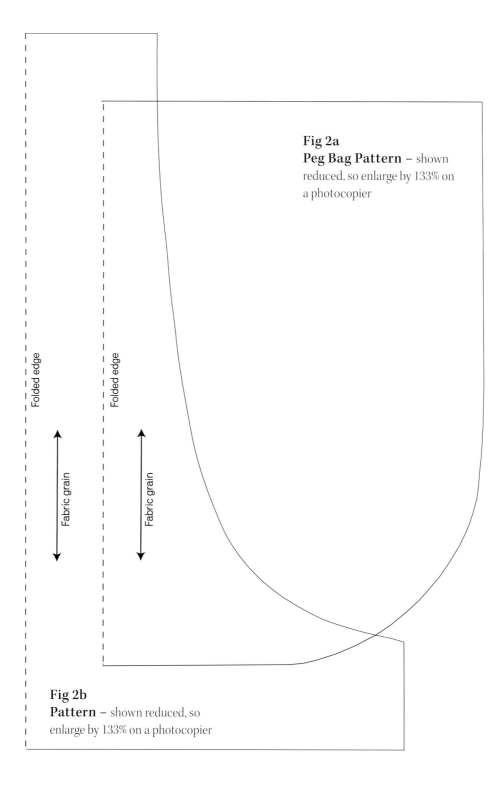

Folded edge

Fabric grain

Folded edge

Fabric grain

Fig 2a
Peg Bag Pattern – shown reduced, so enlarge by 133% on a photocopier

Fig 2b
Pattern – shown reduced, so enlarge by 133% on a photocopier

Fig 6
Pattern – shown reduced so enlarge
by 133% on a photocopier

Fig 7
Pattern (reversed shapes) – shown
reduced so enlarge by 133% on a photocopier
Dashed lines indicate where one appliqué piece
fits under another
Arrows indicate fabric grain

Daisy Chain

I designed this simple daisy block as part of a commissioned quilt that I made, and it caught the eye of Joan Webster, one of my regular students. She had a hoard of pink and mauve batik fabrics that she was longing to use, so this design was perfect to create blocks of the Michaelmas daisies which grace so many English gardens each September and October. A selection of very similar green fabrics for the stems and leaves was gathered and she was ready to go. The green used in the alternating chain blocks was found later and chosen to blend with the original collection of leaf fabrics.

Halfway through the quilt a familiar crisis occurred when Joan realized that the couple of yards of white print fabric she was using for the background was not going to be enough for the quilt, which was developing from a lap size design into a proper bed quilt. The whole project was put on hold for months while she trawled quilt shops, the internet, friends and family until she finally was able to track some down and continue with the design. How often does that happen to us all? Of course we had considered strategies for supplementing the original background with a similar fabric and placing the two in an arrangement that looked balanced and part of the planned design, but nothing Joan found seemed to work well, so she just gritted her teeth and continued the quest until happily her efforts were rewarded. So, if you wish to be spared Joan's pain, for this bed quilt project please do note the amount of fabric needed for the background and make sure that you have enough of it at the start.

Daisy Chain Quilt

When a repeat appliqué design is used in a quilt it can lose some of its impact if used in every single block, so here the daisy design is alternated with a favourite of mine that uses four-patch blocks and nine-patch blocks in an Irish Chain effect (see Fig 1 below). When combined with the appliqué blocks the squares form a series of diagonal chains across the quilt, which frame and separate the daisy blocks. The same 9in (22.9cm) square chain block could be combined with one of the other appliqué designs in this book to create a completely different quilt. The blocks of appliqué and squares are alternated to make the main quilt which is then simply and effectively framed with three borders. The quilting is also kept simple – a line of machine stitches running across the chains of squares and hand quilting to outline the appliquéd flowers.

Requirements

- Background fabric 3¼yd (3m)

- Assorted pink/mauve fabrics for flowers ½yd/m in total

- Assorted green fabrics for leaves and stems ½yd/m in total

- Scraps of yellow fabric for the flower centres, about 12in (30.5cm) square in total

- Green fabric for the chain blocks and first border 1½yd/m

- Fabric for second flowery border ¾yd/m

- Fabric for outer mauve border 1yd/m

- Wadding (batting) 95in x 65in (241.3cm x 165cm)

- Backing fabric 95in x 65in (241.3cm x 165cm)

- Binding fabric from joined short lengths of the pink and mauve daisy fabrics ½yd/m in total

- Fusible web 2yd/m (if using 17in/43.2cm wide type)

- Threads for blanket stitch

Size of finished blocks:

9in x 9in (22.9cm x 22.9cm)

Size of finished quilt:

93in x 63in (236.2cm x 160cm)

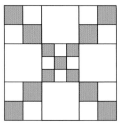

Fig 1

TIP

Because this is quite a complex design, I would recommend using either a see-through appliqué pressing sheet or sheets of non-stick parchment baking paper when building up each daisy design (see Tools for the Task: Fusible Web).

Making One Daisy Appliqué Block

1 Each daisy appliqué block needs a square of background fabric measuring 9½in x 9½in (24.1cm x 24.1cm). For this quilt you will need seventeen pieces of background fabric this size, one for each block. You may like to cut all the background squares at this stage ready to use, or cut each piece as you need it – your choice. In addition, six pieces of background fabric cut 9½in x 6½in (24.1cm x 16.5cm) need to be cut for the part-blocks used at the top and bottom of the quilt.

2 **Choosing the fabrics:** Use the patterns given at the end of the project instructions. The daisy design can be seen full size in Fig 2. Each block has three daisies plus a bud, with green stems and leaves. You may decide, like Joan, to mix the pink and mauve fabrics for each block, varying them in each arrangement so that no two blocks are the same. Alternatively, you could place the colours in the same position for every block. Joan used one green fabric for the stems and another for the leaves in each block, varying the fabrics in each arrangement. The photograph here shows how Joan used her fabrics to create the daisy design.

3 **Tracing the design:** When using a fusible web the design must be reversed. Fig 3 gives each reversed shape to make the daisy design. The dashed lines should be included – they are the areas where one shape is overlapped by another. Place the fusible web smooth side *uppermost* over the fifteen shapes in Fig 3. Follow the instructions given in Essential Techniques: Using Fusible Web to trace and cut out the required shapes from fusible web. Remove the inner section of fusible web from pieces 2 and 10 (two large daisies) and from pieces 13, 14 and 15 (three large leaves). Leave all other shapes whole, as cutting away the inner areas is too fiddly. When the inner area is cut from pieces 2 and 10, the flower centres (pieces 3 and 11) which are drawn in this area will now be ready to cut out in the same way.

4 Take the fabrics chosen for the design. Place each cut piece of fusible web with the rough side *downwards* on the *wrong* side of each chosen fabric, matching the grain line arrow with the grain or weave of the fabric. Follow the instructions given in Essential Techniques: Using Fusible Web to iron the fusible web in place and to cut out each piece of the design.

5 **Building up the design:** You will need to work on an ironing surface to position each piece, so at this stage trace the whole design from Fig 2 clearly on to thin paper or tracing paper – alternatively, photocopy it to save time and energy. Cut a piece of non-stick parchment baking paper a little larger than the finished design shown in Fig 2 or use a see-through appliqué pressing sheet.

6 Place the paper or pressing sheet over your copy of Fig 2 on the ironing surface. Fix both layers in place on the surface with pins or masking tape at the corners. Starting with piece 1 (shortest stem), remove the paper backing. Position the stem right side up, glue side down in the correct place on the parchment paper or pressing sheet. Press lightly with the iron to stick it on to the paper or sheet. Alternatively, you can arrange the entire design and make any final adjustments before ironing anything. A final pressing of the whole piece will fix the design in place on the paper or pressing sheet.

7 Place piece 2 (large daisy) in position, overlapping the end of the stem slightly, and iron in place. Position the daisy centre (piece 3) on to the flower and press.

8 In the same way position pieces 4, 5 and 6, using the drawing of Fig 2 beneath as a guide. Iron in place. The daisy (piece 5) should overlap the end of the stem (piece 4) and the flower centre (piece 6) should overlap the flower as shown by the dashed lines on the pieces in Fig 3.

9 Repeat this process with the daisy bud (pieces 7 and 8) and the other large daisy (pieces 9, 10 and 11) using the original drawing of Fig 2 as a guide.

10 Finally, arrange the four leaves (12, 13, 14 and 15) and press the whole design firmly with a hot iron to fix all the pieces in place on the background fabric.

11 **Stitching the design:** Joan stitched the design by hand, using a slightly thicker thread than usual, but if you wish to machine stitch it, that will be fine. She used Gütermann silk thread, using green thread to outline the stems and leaves and pink and mauve shades for the flowers. You might prefer to use a variegated thread, or follow the traditional route and outline the whole design with black thread. See Tools for the Task: Threads and Needles for more information on your choices. For blanket stitching refer to Essential Techniques: Blanket Stitching by Hand or Blanket Stitching by Machine. I would stitch around the flowers first, then the stems and finish with the leaves, but you may prefer a different order of stitching.

12 I often cut away the back layers after blanket stitching to reduce the thicknesses for quilting but on this occasion Joan chose to leave the background layers in place to give the design more stability.

Making More Blocks

Making the first block always takes a long time: trying out stitches and threads, choosing fabrics, mastering the nuances of the design and so on. Once this block is completed, it becomes your reference for all those decisions made as you worked on it and making the others becomes far easier. If you are varying the fabrics from block to block, keep the finished blocks in view as you select the fabrics for the next daisy design – this will give an overview of the growing collection and ensure that the colours are evenly distributed in the quilt.

Making the Chain Blocks

1 Eighteen blocks are needed for the quilt, plus four part-blocks added at the top and bottom of the quilt to extend them a little. From background fabric cut eighty-four squares each 3½in x 3½in (8.9cm x 8.9cm).

Making the Four-Patch Blocks

2 Eighty four-patch blocks are needed for the quilt. From the green fabric chosen for the chain squares cut strips each 2in (5.1cm) wide and in a length totalling about 9yd (8.25m) – see Tip below.

TIP

If you cut your strips down the length of the 1½yd or metres of green fabric, parallel to the woven selvedge edge, you will need six strips all 2in (5.1cm) wide to make all the four-patch blocks. If you cut the strips across the fabric from selvedge to selvedge (the woven side edges of the fabric), you will need nine strips all 2in (5.1cm) wide.

3 From the background fabric cut the same number of strips 2in (5.1cm) wide and in a length to match the strips cut from the green fabric.

4 Place a strip of green fabric with a similar strip of background fabric, right sides facing. Stitch a ¼in (6mm) seam to join the strips together, matching edges carefully and using a smaller stitch length than usual (Fig 4). Open the strips out and press the seam towards the green fabric, ironing from the front (Fig 5). In the same way, stitch all the remaining strips into pairs, pressing the seam towards the green fabric each time.

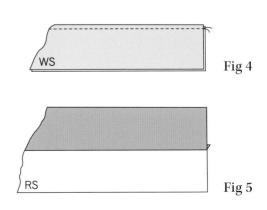

WS
Fig 4

RS
Fig 5

TIP

The joined strips should measure 3½in (8.9cm) wide at this stage. Stitch the first pair together and check the width – if it is not this measurement, adjust the seam allowance until it is correct. I often move the needle on my machine slightly to the right, making the distance from the needle to the edge of the quarter-inch foot a scant ¼in (6mm), which works best for most patchwork piecing. Once you are achieving an accurate seam allowance, stitch the rest of the strips into pairs.

5 Cut the joined strips vertically into 2in (5.1cm) wide pieces (Fig 6).

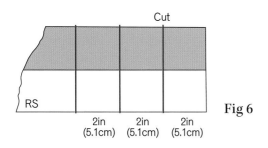

Cut

RS

2in (5.1cm) 2in (5.1cm) 2in (5.1cm)

Fig 6

6 In the same way, continue to stitch pairs of strips together and cut them into pieces until 160 pieces have been cut.

7 Arrange two of the cut pieces into a four-patch as shown in Fig 7. Pin and stitch the pair together, matching the centre seams carefully. Press the seam to one side, ironing from the front (Fig 8). The four-patch should measure 3½in (8.9cm) square at this stage.

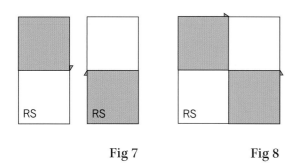

RS   RS   RS

Fig 7   **Fig 8**

8 Continue to pin and stitch each four-patch block until eighty are made. Time and thread can be saved if the blocks are stitched in a chain, one after the other, without taking them off the machine and cutting threads between each block once they are completed.

Making the Nine-Patch Blocks

9 Twenty-two nine-patch blocks are needed for the quilt. From the green fabric chosen for the chain squares cut five strips each 1½in (3.8cm) wide and 34in (86.4cm) long. Cut four strips of background fabric in the same measurements.

10 Arrange two strips of the green fabric and one strip of background fabric as Fig 9a. Pin and stitch the three strips together with a scant ¼in (6mm) seam. Alternate the direction of stitching the strips to help keep the band flat and not rippled. Press from the front, ironing both seams towards the green fabric (Fig 9b). This is Band A. Repeat this process with a second set of strips to make an identical Band A as in Fig 9b.

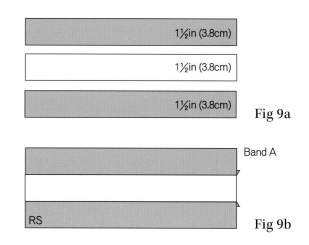

1½in (3.8cm)

1½in (3.8cm)

1½in (3.8cm)   **Fig 9a**

Band A

RS   **Fig 9b**

11 Take the remaining three strips and arrange them as in Fig 10a. Pin and stitch the strips together as before. Press the seams from the front towards the green fabric (Fig 10b). This is Band B.

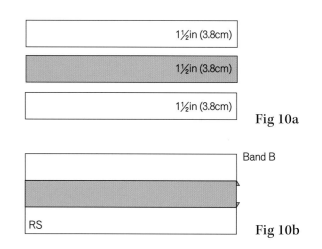

1½in (3.8cm)

1½in (3.8cm)

1½in (3.8cm)   **Fig 10a**

Band B

RS   **Fig 10b**

12 From each stitched band, cut twenty-two pieces each 1½in (3.8cm) wide, making a total of forty-four cut pieces of Band A and twenty-two cut pieces of Band B (Fig 11).

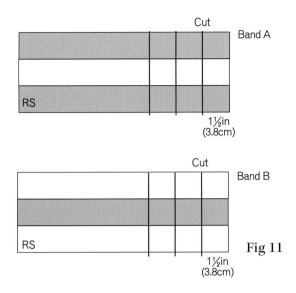

Fig 11

13 Take two pieces from Band A and one piece from Band B and arrange as Fig 12. Pin and stitch the pieces together, matching seams carefully. Press the two vertical seams away from the centre of the block as Fig 13. Assemble the other twenty-one nine-patch blocks in the same way, chaining the pieces as described before.

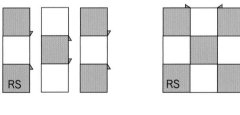

Fig 12   Fig 13

Assembling the Chain Blocks

14 Arrange four background squares (3½in/8.9cm) with four four-patch blocks and one nine-patch block as in Fig 14. Pin and stitch the top row of three units together and press seams towards the background square (Fig 15a). Pin and stitch the second row together and press the seams towards the background (Fig 15b). Pin and stitch the bottom row and press as the top row (Fig 15c). Finally, pin and stitch the three rows together, matching seams carefully. Press the two long seams to one side, ironing from the front.

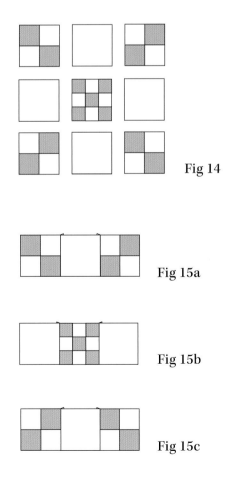

Fig 14

Fig 15a

Fig 15b

Fig 15c

15 Assemble eighteen complete chain blocks. The remaining units are used to make four part-blocks as shown in Fig 16. These will be used at the top and bottom of the quilt when all the blocks are joined together.

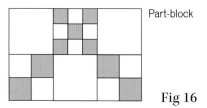

Part-block

Fig 16

16 To make a part-block, take three background squares, two four-patch blocks and one nine-patch block and arrange them in two rows as in Fig 17. Stitch them into two rows, pressing the seams as described in step 14. Finally, join the rows together, matching seams carefully. Press the final long seam to one side. Make three more of these part-blocks – four in total.

Fig 18a

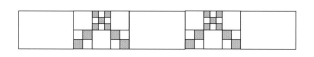

Fig 18b

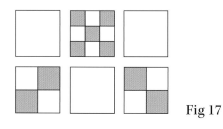

Fig 17

Fig 18c

Assembling the Quilt

1 Arrange the thirty-five complete blocks into seven rows each of five blocks as in Fig 18a.

2 To make the part-blocks for the top and bottom an extra six pieces of background fabric will be needed, each measuring 9½in x 6½in (24.1cm x 16.5cm). Arrange the top row of three background pieces and two chain part-blocks as in Fig 18b. Arrange the bottom row of part-blocks as in Fig 18c.

3 Pin and stitch the top part-block row together with the usual ¼in (6mm) seam. Press seams to one side, ironing from the front.

4 Pin and stitch the second row of five blocks together. Press the seams in the opposite direction to those of the first row, ironing from the front. Continue to pin and stitch each row, pressing seams in alternate directions to help to lock them. Finally, join the bottom row of part-blocks to complete the design.

5 Join the seven rows together, matching seams carefully. Press seams to one side, ironing from the front.

Adding the Borders

6 Measure the quilt across its centre in both directions. It should measure 45½in (115.6cm) from side to side and 75½in (191.8cm) from top to bottom at this stage.

TIP

If your quilt does not match these measurements, don't worry – just use your own measurements for the length of the border strips and that will be fine.

7 **Adding the inner border:** From the green chain fabric cut two strips each 2½in (6.4cm) wide and 75½in (191.8cm) long (or a measurement to match the length of your quilt). Pin and stitch these to either side of the quilt. Press seams outwards, away from the quilt.

8 Measure across the centre of the quilt from side to side. It should now measure 49½in (125.7cm). From the same fabric cut two strips 2½in (6.4cm) wide and 49½in (125.7cm) long (or a length to match your own quilt measurement). Pin and stitch these strips to the top and bottom of the quilt. Press the seams outwards, away from the quilt.

9 **Adding the middle border:** Measure down the centre of the quilt from top to bottom. Cut two strips from the chosen fabric 3½in (8.9cm) wide and a length to match your quilt. Pin and stitch these to either side of the quilt. Press the seams outwards as before.

10 Measure across the centre of the quilt from side to side. From the same border fabric cut two strips 3½in (8.9cm) wide and a length to match the width of the quilt. Pin and stitch these strips to the top and bottom of the quilt. Press the seams outwards.

11 **Adding the outer border:** Repeat the process with the fabric chosen for the outer border, cutting the four strips 4in (10.2cm) wide and in lengths to match the quilt. Press seams outwards as before.

Quilting and Finishing

12 Layer the quilt with wadding (batting) and backing fabric – see Quilting. Refer to the Requirements list for the sizes of these. Joan kept the quilting simple to complement the classic design of her quilt. She quilted by machine diagonally through the green squares of the chain blocks and used a decorative stitch along the seams of the framing borders on the quilt. She then hand quilted around the appliquéd flowers and leaves and added more hand quilting in the large areas of white background fabric at the top and bottom of the quilt.

13 To bind the quilt, short lengths of all the pink and mauve fabrics used for the daisies were joined together to make a multi-fabric binding, which echoed the design of the appliqué blocks in the quilt beautifully. Refer to Binding a Quilt.

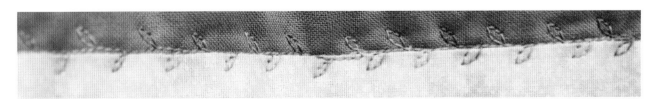

Patterns

Fig 2
Pattern – shown full size

Fig 3
Pattern Pieces (reversed design)–
shown full size
Dashed lines indicate where one appliqué
piece fit under another

Flower Lattice

Some years ago when I was designing paint stencils for an American company (and that's another story...) I spent a lot of time researching old stencils that were used as chapter headings in old books. I had planned to adapt this Victorian stencil at the time, but somehow it never worked out. The years went by and here I am now focusing on designs suitable for blanket stitch appliqué, and this time round the design seems just right. The combination of soft rounded flowers and leaves in the centre framed in a formal lattice arrangement seems to work so well in this charming quilt design.

The start of it all was a metre of fabric brought back from Australia as a gift from one of my regular students, Mavis Hall. Just as I favour soft muted colours, so Mavis works with bright fabrics – reds, yellows and all the primaries. This gift was to prove to me that she could choose and even buy fabric that was out of her own comfort zone, knowing that I would love it. How right she was! A metre of dappled greys, mauves and the palest of pinks – I loved it immediately and having spent some months just stroking it and crooning to myself I was ready to use it. Carefully cut, it produced the nine background squares to the flower and lattice blocks, with practically nothing left over. Everything else used was chosen to blend and enhance the pastel effect which gives me so much pleasure. It could also look wonderful with vibrant batiks or the rich dark shades of Civil War fabrics, so don't feel the design is limited to the delicate look shown here. As always, start with a collection of fabrics you are longing to use, cut out and prepare one block and get stitching.

Flower Lattice Quilt

The nine flower and lattice blocks for this quilt were made as separate 12in x 12in (30.5cm x 30.5cm) finished squares, each of which was appliquéd with the design before being joined together to make the centre of the quilt. Two shades of pink were used for the flowers and the tendrils in each block, plus a grey-blue for the leaves. It would be quite possible of course to make a larger bed quilt by making more blocks for the centre area if you wished. The centre blocks were framed with a blue border quilted in a series of channels that echo the lattice strips of the blocks, and then a wide strip of blanket-stitched pieces were added to enclose the main design, like a pebble path around a formal garden. I had to choose a second fabric for the pebble path background in my quilt, but ideally I would have used just the one fabric. A final blue border quilted in channels like the inner border completes the quilt.

Requirements

- Background fabric for the nine appliquéd blocks and for background strips for the pebble path border 1¾yd/m

- Two fabrics (A and B) for the flowers in the appliqué blocks ½yd/m of each (also used in the pebble path border)

- Fabric for leaves in the appliqué blocks plus first border ¾yd/m (also used in the pebble path border)

- Assorted scraps of at least five fabrics to add to the appliqué fabrics to make the appliquéd pebbles

- Fabric for final border and binding 1½yd/m – if you are prepared to have joins you could manage with 1yd/m

- Wadding (batting) 56in x 56in (142.2cm x 142.2cm)

- Backing fabric 56in x 56in (142.2cm x 142.2cm)

- Fusible web 3yd/m (if using 17in/43.2cm wide)

- Threads for blanket stitch

Size of finished block:

12in x 12in (30.5cm x 30.5cm)

Size of finished quilt:

54in x 54in (137.2cm x 137.2cm)

TIP

If you are planning to make a larger quilt from this design, you might like to alternate the flower appliqué block with a simpler block, or even combine it with a quilted version, as Judy Baker-Rogers did with her Art Deco Rose quilt.

Making One Appliqué Block

1 Each appliqué flower and lattice block needs a cut piece of background fabric measuring 12½in x 12½in (31.8cm x 31.8cm). For this quilt you will need nine pieces of background fabric this size, one for each appliqué block. You may like to cut all the background squares at this stage ready to use, or cut each piece as you need it.

2 **Transferring the design to the fabric:** Use the patterns at the end of the project instructions, enlarging them as described there. To make a master copy of the centre flower design, trace the *whole* design on to paper, using the parts of Fig 2, matching up the dashed blue lines and referring to Fig 1 below. The edging lattice strips are dealt with later. Fold the square of background fabric lightly into four. Use the fold lines as a guide for positioning the central flower design – the dashed lines on the master copy should match the fold lines on the background fabric. Mark the appliqué pattern on the *right* side of the background fabric square by tracing the design, using a sharp marking pencil and light box if necessary. The traced lines are a guide for positioning the cut pieces of appliqué fabric, so trace lightly just *inside* the drawn line so these lines will be hidden when the appliqué shapes are placed over them. If the fabric is too dark for the design to be traced through, use dressmaker's carbon paper and a tracing wheel. (I use an empty fine ballpoint pen to mark the design through the carbon paper.)

TIP

If your background fabric is light in colour and the master copy is made with a strong drawn line, you might not have to trace the outlines on to the background fabric. Instead, after preparing and cutting out all the pieces for the design ready for assembly on the background, place the master copy on the ironing board and pin the background fabric right side *up* over it on the board. If you can see the shapes on the master copy clearly through the fabric, use these as a guide for positioning each piece of appliqué on the background and ironing it in place.

3 **Tracing the pieces:** When using fusible web, the design must be reversed. Three fabrics are used in each block for the appliqué, so I have grouped together the pieces needed for each fabric. Fig 3a gives the pieces that make the larger flower, both flower centres and the tendrils, all cut from flower fabric A. Fig 3b gives the smaller flower without its centre, cut from flower fabric B. Fig 3c gives the leaves, all cut from the chosen leaf fabric. Trace the shapes in Fig 3a on to the smooth side of the fusible web. Mark the numbers and grain line arrows on the tracing, keeping these at the very edge of each shape, as the centre part of fusible web may be removed later.

4 From the traced design, cut out the flower pattern in one piece (which includes the numbered shapes 1–7) roughly just beyond the drawn lines to separate it from the rest of the design (Fig 4a). Now carefully cut about ⅛in (3mm) *inside* the drawn lines of shapes 2, 3, 4, 5, 6 and 7 (Fig 4b). Do not attempt to cut away inside piece 1 as it is just too small and fiddly. Cut out the smaller pieces (the second flower centre and the five tendrils) by cutting each one roughly just beyond the drawn lines. These are also too small to cut away inside the drawn lines.

Fig 1

Fig 4a   **Fig 4b**

5 Place these pieces of fusible web rough side *down* on the *wrong* side of the fabric chosen for the larger flower, matching the grain line arrows with the grain or weave of the fabric. Follow the instructions given in Essential Techniques: Using Fusible Web to iron the fusible web in place and to cut out each piece of the design, to make the seven segments of the flower plus the second flower centre (piece 13) and tendrils (pieces 8, 9, 10, 11 and 12).

6 Trace the shapes in Fig 3b (shapes 14–19), the smaller flower, on to the smooth side of the fusible web, following steps 4 and 5 above and ironing the whole flower shape on to the wrong side of the fabric chosen for the smaller flower. Cut out each shape on the drawn lines.

7 Trace the five shapes in Fig 3c (pieces 20–24) on to fusible web. Label each piece as usual with the number and grain line. Cut away the web inside each shape as described above. Follow step 5 to make each of the five leaf shapes ready for use in the design.

8 **Building up the centre design:** Remove the backing paper from each of the pieces. Arrange the two flowers in position on the background fabric, right side *up*, glue side *down*, taking care that each piece covers the drawn outline on the square of background fabric. When you are happy with the arrangement, press everything with a hot iron to fix the pieces in place. In the same way add the leaves and tendrils in their positions on the background fabric and iron them in place.

9 **Adding the lattice strips:** The four strips used to make the lattice are shown in Fig 5a and given in reversed form ready for tracing in Fig 5b. Trace each shape four times on to fusible web in the usual way, including the numbers L1, L2, L3 and L4 and the grain line arrow. Cut each piece out roughly – do not remove any of the fusible web from within each strip as they are too narrow. Follow steps 4 and 5 above to make each of the sixteen strips ready for adding to the design.

10 Mark a line ¾in (1.9cm) from the outer edge of the background square of fabric on all four sides (Fig 6). Do this with a chalk-based marking pencil or a

hera – the line needs to be temporary, as it is a guide for positioning the lattice pieces and would spoil the final design if a permanent marker was used.

Fig 6

11 Remove the backing paper just from the four strips marked (L1). Work on the ironing board and using Fig 5a as a guide position one of these strips at the top left corner of the marked guideline, matching the corner of the strip with the corner of the guideline as in Fig 7a. Press with the iron to fix it in place. Turn the block through 90 degrees and place another strip marked (L1) at the top left corner of the marked guideline as before (Fig 7b). Repeat this at each corner of the guideline, turning the block each time so that the arrangement is repeated exactly on each side (Fig 7c).

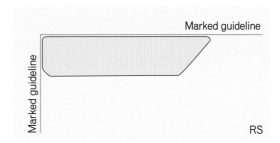

Fig 7a

Fig 7b

Fig 7c

12 Use the marked guideline on the background fabric and Fig 5a to help position the other strips. There should be about ¼in (6mm) between one strip and the next one. The complete lattice arrangement is shown in Fig 8. Once you are happy with the placing of the pieces, press with the iron to fix the strips in place.

Fig 8

13 **Stitching the design:** I stitched my design by hand, using Gütermann silk thread in colours matching the appliqué fabrics but slightly stronger to give the shapes more definition. If you wish to machine stitch it, that will be fine. See Tools for the Task: Threads and Needles for more information. For stitching either by hand or machine, refer to Essential Techniques: Blanket Stitching by Hand or Blanket Stitching by Machine. I suggest you start by stitching around the flowers before moving on to the leaves, leaving the smaller tendrils until last. You may prefer a different order of stitching.

14 I often cut away the back layers after blanket stitching to reduce the thicknesses for quilting, but for this design where the pieces do not overlap each other, the appliqué fabrics are stabilized by leaving all the layers intact.

15 Once you are happy with your first appliquéd block, continue to make a total of nine blocks.

16 **Joining the blocks:** Measure each block – each one should be 12½in x 12½in (31.8cm x 31.8cm) but may have distorted a little with the stitching of the

appliqué. If it needs to be reduced a little to square it up this won't matter, as long as all the blocks finish up the same size. I trimmed my blocks down slightly on all sides so that the lattice strips were a little closer together when the blocks were joined. Arrange the blocks in three rows with three blocks in each row. The design can be arranged in exactly the same way in every block or try turning the blocks each time so that the flowers are in different positions on the blocks, as I did in my quilt.

17 Once you have found the arrangement that you like best, pin and stitch the top row of blocks together with the usual ¼in (6mm) seam. Press the seams to one side, ironing from the front of the work. Repeat this with the second row, pressing the seams in the opposite direction to those in the first row. Finally, stitch the bottom row together, pressing the seams in the opposite direction to the middle row of blocks.

18 Pin and stitch the three rows together, matching seams carefully and pressing seams to one side, ironing from the front.

Adding the Borders

1 **Adding the first border:** Measure the quilt across its centre in both directions. It should measure 36½in (92.7cm) in both directions. Don't worry if your quilt isn't this measurment – just cut the strips in a length to match your quilt. From the fabric used for the lattice strips cut two strips each 2½in (6.4cm) wide and 36½in (92.7cm) long, or a length to match your quilt measurement.

2 Pin and stitch a cut strip to either side of the quilt. Press the seams outwards, away from the quilt, ironing from the front (Fig 9a).

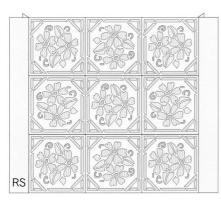

Fig 9a

3 Measure across the quilt from side to side. From the fabric used for the lattice strips cut two strips each 2½in (6.4cm) wide and a length to match your quilt.

4 Pin and stitch a strip to the top and bottom of the quilt (Fig 9b). Press the seams outwards.

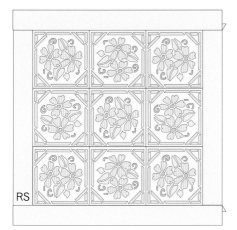

Fig 9b

5 **Adding the second border:** Measure your quilt across the centre – it should measure 40½in (102.9cm) in both directions, but use your own quilt's measurements if they are different to this. From the fabric chosen for the background to the pebble path border cut four strips each 4½in (11.4cm) wide and a length to match your quilt measurement. Also cut four squares of the same fabric for the cornerstones of the border, each 4½in x 4½in (11.4cm x 11.4cm).

6 **Making the pebble appliqué:** The pebbles on each side of the quilt are made from the block of pebbles shown in Fig 10a repeated twelve times on each long strip of background fabric. A square block of pebbles is used on each cornerstone square of the background fabric (Fig 10b). The pieces do not need to be reversed for tracing with fusible web as they are the same on either side. It is easier to handle if the appliqué pieces are stitched in place on the background strips before joining to the main quilt. Begin by making just one side of the border. Trace the four pebbles from Fig 10a twelve times each on to the shiny side of fusible web. Cut out each shape roughly and remove the inner section of the web from each shape. Iron the shapes on to the back of as many fabrics as you have collected for the pebbles, including fabrics used in the flower appliqués. Cut out the shapes and remove the paper backing ready to arrange the pebbles on the background strip.

7 To help position the pebbles, fold a strip of background fabric in half and crease it well to mark the centre. Fold once more and crease again to mark the strip in four sections (Fig 11).

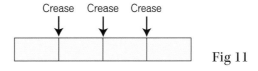

Fig 11

8 Arrange three blocks of pebbles as shown in Fig 10a on the strip, leaving about ¼in (6mm) between each of the pebbles. Keep the pieces about ⅜in (1cm) from the top and bottom long edges of the background strips on the background fabric. Begin about ⅜in (1cm) from the end of the strip and finish ⅛in (3mm) from the first marked crease on the strip (Fig 12a).

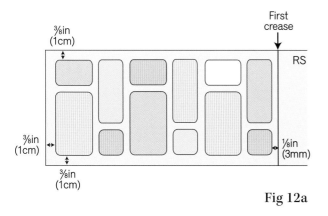

Fig 12a

TIP

Resist the temptation to iron the pebbles in place as you go along, as some overall adjustments might have to be made, especially if your background strip is shorter than 40½in (102.9cm). Arrange at least as far as halfway along the background strip, when you should be able to judge whether everything is fitting in nicely or whether you may have to juggle a little.

9 Arrange the second section of pebbles on the background strip, finishing ⅛in (3mm) from the halfway crease on the strip (Fig 12b). If all is going well, you can iron the pebbles before arranging the other two sections of pebbles on the strip in the same way. If your strip just isn't long enough to accommodate twelve blocks of pebbles in this way, omit the last two pebbles and arrange the rest evenly along the strip – no one will notice, I promise.

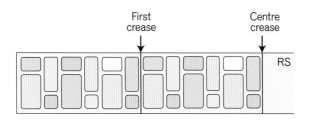

Fig 12b

10 Once you have completed one strip of pebbles, use it as a guide to arrange and stick the pebbles on a second border strip. Or you can leave the cutting and sticking for a while and enjoy stitching around each shape on the first strip either by hand or machine in the usual way before preparing the second strip.

11 Pin and stitch a cornerstone square to either end of the two remaining cut strips (Fig 13). Press the seams towards the long strips.

Fig 13

12 The two long border strips have their pebbles arranged on the main section exactly as the first two, with the addition of the special square block shown in Fig 10b, which is used for the cornerstone squares stitched to either end of these long strips. Trace the four shapes from Fig 10b four times each on to fusible web in the usual way. Follow step 6 above to make the pebble shapes ready for sticking on to the cornerstone squares.

13 Arrange the four pieces on to the cornerstone squares, as shown in Fig 10b, keeping clear of the seam allowances as described previously. Once everything looks good, iron the pieces into place on the background in the usual way ready for stitching.

14 Complete all the blanket stitching on the pebbles before arranging the border strips around the quilt – the two shorter strips are placed against the sides of the quilt and the two longer strips with the cornerstones are placed at the top and bottom of the quilt. Pin and stitch the two side pebble border strips to the quilt. Press the seams outwards, away from the quilt. Pin and stitch the top and bottom pebble border strips to the quilt. Press the seams outwards, away from the quilt.

Quilting and Finishing

19 Layer the quilt with wadding (batting) and backing fabric – see Quilting. I quilted by hand all of the centre area with the nine appliqué blocks, outlining each shape about ⅛in (3mm) away from the blanket-stitched edges of the flower design and the lattice strips. I also quilted parallel lines by hand on the two blue borders and outlined the pebbles in the middle border in the same way as the flower blocks. I used my machine to stitch in the seam lines of each border strip, (known as quilting in the ditch), which only shows at the back of the quilt, so the overall look is of a hand-quilted piece. That was my choice, of course – whether you quilt by hand or machine or a mixture of both is up to you, as is the amount of quilting you wish to have on your quilt.

20 Finally, finish your quilt by binding it in the same fabric as the final border – see Binding a Quilt.

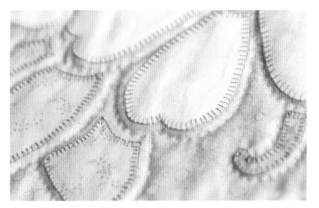

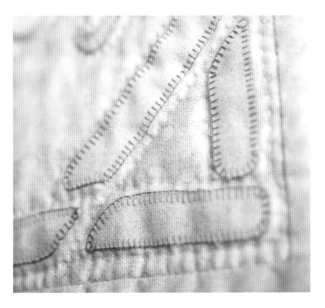

15 **Adding the third border:** Measure the quilt down its centre from top to bottom. From the fabric chosen for the final border and binding cut two strips each 3in (7.6cm) wide and in a length to match your quilt measurement.

16 Pin and stitch a cut strip to either side of the quilt. Press the seams outwards, away from the quilt, ironing from the front.

17 Measure across the quilt from side to side. From the chosen fabric cut two strips each 3in (7.6cm) wide and in a length to match your quilt measurement.

18 Pin and stitch a strip to the top and bottom of the quilt. Press seams outwards.

Patterns

Fig 2
Pattern (left section) – shown reduced, so enlarge by 143% on a photocopier
Dashed blue lines indicate the centre point of the pattern – match up the lines on the two parts of the pattern

Fig 2
Pattern (right section) – shown reduced, so enlarge by 143% on a photocopier

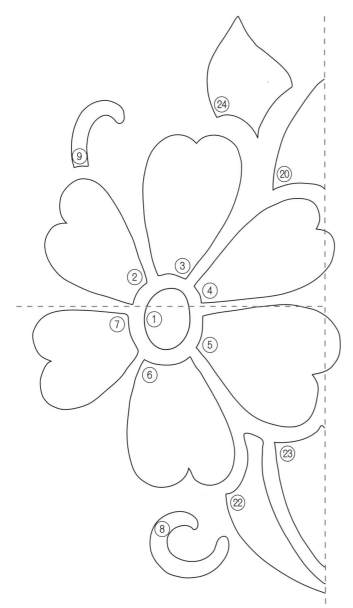

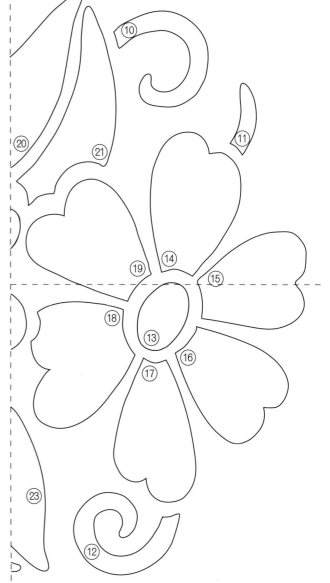

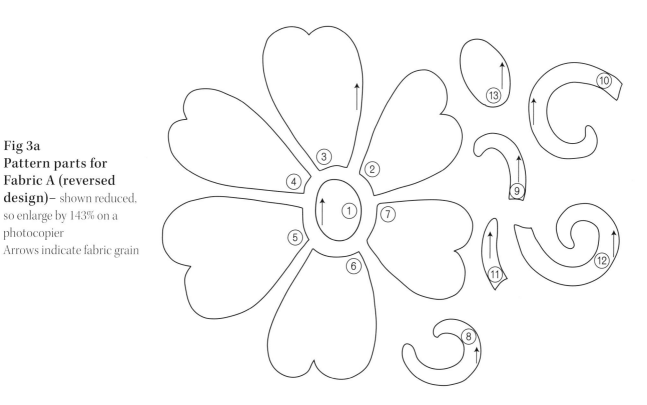

Fig 3a
Pattern parts for Fabric A (reversed design) – shown reduced, so enlarge by 143% on a photocopier
Arrows indicate fabric grain

Fig 3b
Pattern parts for Fabric B (reversed design) – shown reduced, so enlarge by 143% on a photocopier

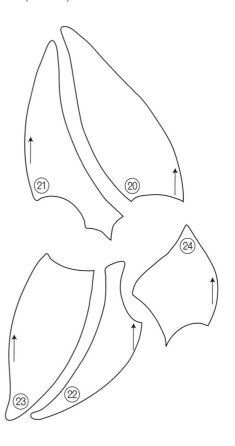

Fig 3c
Pattern parts for Leaf Fabric (reversed design) – shown reduced, so enlarge by 143% on a photocopier

Fig 5a
Lattice Pattern – shown reduced,
so enlarge by 143% on a photocopier

Fig 5b
Lattice Pattern – shown reduced,
so enlarge by 143% on a photocopier
Arrows indicate fabric grain

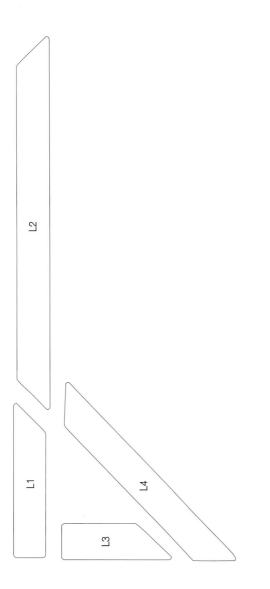

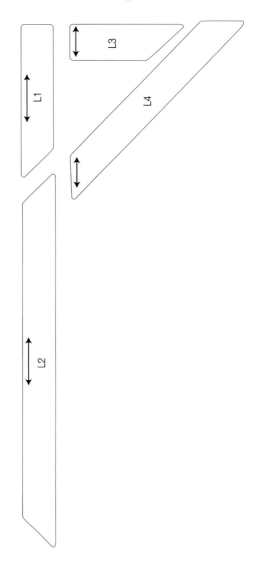

Fig 10a
Pebble Pattern for Border – shown
reduced, so enlarge by 143% on a photocopier
Arrows indicate fabric grain

Fig 10b
Pebble Pattern for Cornerstone Squares –
shown reduced, so enlarge by 143% on a photocopier
Arrows indicate fabric grain

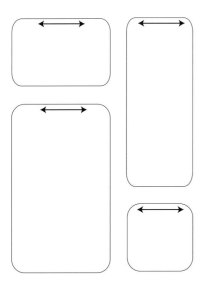

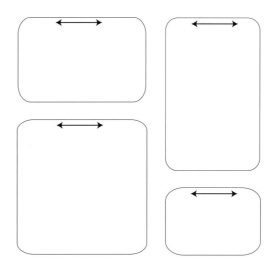

Elephants on Parade

This small quilt could be used as a wall hanging or as a quilt for a child, to be carried around, used on a cot or as a floor quilt for a small baby. If, having toiled over the design, you feel it's really too precious to be used in the rough and tumble of a child's life, stitch a sleeve for hanging it on to the back and give it together with a suitable rod or hanging device – that way you make it easy for the recipient to put it into place straight away. If it is to be a wall decoration, this is your chance to add some exotic embellishment and stitchery to enhance the Eastern feel of the design.

The elephant first appeared as a pieced design that I developed into a wall hanging with a mixture of large and small elephants parading across the quilt. It appeared as a project in a magazine and seemed very popular – but not, apparently, with everyone... One of my regular students, Julia Reed, preferred to make an appliquéd elephant as opposed to a pieced one, so she swiftly adapted my design, blanket stitched it on to a background fabric and made it into a panel for a bag. I try not to encourage my students to use their initiative, preferring slavish obedience, but sometimes this wilful behaviour can be turned to my advantage, as here. Julia's appliqué adaptation worked so well that I immediately adopted it, and I have had so much fun interpreting the blanket-stitched version into the exotic Eastern elephant quilt project described here.

The delightful original bag made by Julia that started it all is described after the wall hanging project. The baby elephant appliqué is just the perfect size for the panels on the bag, and has proved to be a real favourite with the keen bag-makers in my classes.

Elephant Parade Wall Hanging

This wall-hung quilt uses two sizes of elephant, three large and six small. These are arranged on three wide strips of background fabric, with three elephants appliquéd on to each piece of background in each row, positioned in alternating directions. The horizontal rows are separated and framed with a narrow strip of contrast fabric and the whole design is bordered with an appliquéd triangular design in the style of traditional Indian textiles. I wanted to add to the exotic flavour by choosing fabrics in rich and vibrant shades, with mauves and purples contrasting with the bright teal background, but an equally effective quilt could be made using more naturalistic colours of course. Other exotic animal designs could be used in this project – try looking in children's colouring books for simple outline shapes that could be adapted for appliqué designs.

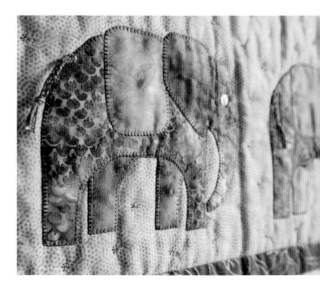

Requirements

- Four shades of mauve/purple batik fabrics (two for the large elephants and two for the smaller), a fat quarter of each fabric

- Fabric for all saddle cloths and head cloths plus strips for the final border ½yd/m

- Background fabric for the elephants plus final binding 1yd/m

- Fabric for narrow framing strips ⅜yd (35cm)

- Fat quarter of fabric for border appliqué

- Wadding (batting) 36in x 34in (91.4cm x 86.4cm)

- Backing fabric 36in x 34in (91.4cm x 86.4cm)

- Fusible web 1yd/m (if using 17in/43.2cm wide type)

- Threads for the blanket stitch

- Yarn or thick thread for elephant tails

- Beads or sequins (optional)

Size of finished block:

larger elephant about 7½in x 6½in (19.1cm x 16.6cm)
smaller elephant about 6¼in x 5¼in (15.9cm x 13.3cm)

Size of quilt:

34½in x 32½in (87.6cm x 82.6cm)

TIP

Because the elephants are arranged by eye on each background strip of fabric. I would recommend using either a see-through appliqué pressing sheet or sheets of non-stick parchment baking paper when building up each elephant. Once completed, they can be removed from the paper or pressing sheet and placed as desired on the background fabric (see Tools for the Task).

Making One Elephant

1 From the background fabric cut three strips, each 26in x 9in (66cm x 22.9cm). There are two sizes of elephant, so start with the larger version.

2 **Tracing the design:** the elephant design is shown in Fig 1 but when using a fusible web the design must be reversed so Fig 2 gives each reversed shape to make the large elephant. Enlarge the patterns as described on the pattern pages. The dashed lines should be included – they are the areas where one shape is overlapped by another. Place the fusible web smooth side *uppermost* over the six shapes in Fig 2. Follow the general instructions for tracing and cutting out the required shapes from the fusible web in Essential Techniques: Using Fusible Web. Remove the inner section of fusible web from every piece except from piece 6, which is just too small and fiddly. When the inner area is cut from piece 3, pieces 4 and 6 (the pieces for the saddle cloth and head cloth), which are drawn within this area, will now be ready to cut out in the same way.

3 Take the two fabrics chosen for the large elephants. One fabric is used for the main body and the other for the two inner legs and ear. Place each cut piece of fusible web with the rough side *downwards* on the *wrong* side of each chosen fabric, matching the grain line arrow with the grain or weave of the fabric. Follow the instructions in Using Fusible Web to iron the fusible web in place and to cut out each piece of the design.

4 **Building up the design:** Work on an ironing surface to position each piece, tracing the whole design from Fig 1 on to thin paper or tracing paper (or photocopy). Cut non-stick parchment baking paper a little larger than the finished design in Fig 1 or use a see-through appliqué pressing sheet.

5 Place the paper or pressing sheet over your copy of Fig 1 on the ironing surface. Fix both layers in place with pins or masking tape at the corners. Starting with pieces 1 and 2 (inner legs), remove the paper backing. Position the legs right side *up*, glue side *down* in the correct place on the parchment paper or pressing sheet. Press lightly with the iron to stick it on to the paper or sheet. Alternatively, arrange the entire design and make any final adjustments before ironing anything. A final pressing of the whole piece will fix the design in place.

6 Place piece 3 (the elephant body) in position and iron in place. Arrange pieces 4 and 5 together on the elephant before ironing them in place. First, position the ear (piece 5), following the drawn outline for the top edge. Then tuck the saddle cloth (piece 4) under the ear on the left side as shown in Fig 1 before pressing both pieces with the iron. Finally, use Fig 1 as a guide to position the head cloth and iron in place.

7 Gently peel the completed design from the paper or pressing sheet and set aside. It's best to make at least the top row of elephants before you start to fix and stitch them to the background strips.

8 **Making a small elephant:** Use the drawn design in Fig 3 and the reversed version for the fusible web in Fig 4, enlarging them as described. Use the other two elephant fabrics for the design plus the same saddle cloth and head cloth fabric as used before. Follow steps 2–7 above to make one small elephant. Repeat to make a second small one. The top row is now ready to assemble on a background strip.

9 Place the three elephants on a strip of background fabric cut 26in x 9in (66cm x 22.9cm), with the large elephant in the lead at the left-hand end. Space the three evenly on the strip. Iron the elephants to fix them in place on the background fabric.

TIP

I marked a line with a hera on the background fabric 1½in (3.8cm) from the bottom long edge. I used this as a marker to position the elephant feet to keep them level. You could place them in a less formal arrangement, in which case you won't need to mark a guideline.

10 The second row of three elephants is facing in the opposite direction. The original Figs 1, 2, 3 and 4 need to be traced, turned over and retraced to use as the patterns for both large and small elephants. Make another one large and two small elephants from these patterns, following steps 2–9 above and arrange them on a strip of background fabric to make the middle row.

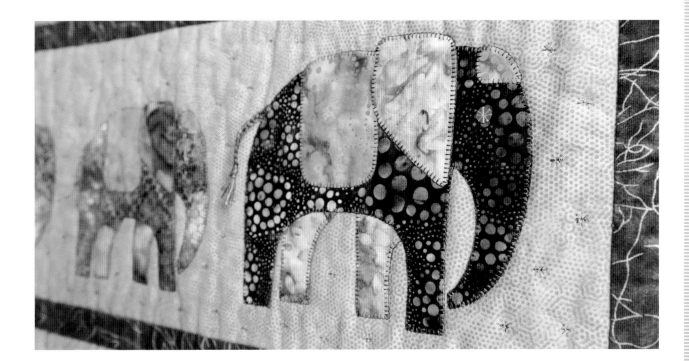

11 Finally, repeat steps 2–9 using the original patterns from Figs 1, 2, 3 and 4 to make a third row exactly the same as row 1.

12 Stitching the design: I stitched around each elephant in blanket stitch by machine, using a purple variegated thread throughout, but whether you stitch by hand or machine is your choice. For information on blanket stitching refer to Essential Techniques: Blanket Stitching by Hand and Blanket Stitching by Machine. See also Tools for the Task: Threads and Needles. I first stitched around the saddle cloth and ear in one unit to avoid stopping and starting too often and ending up with lots of thread ends to deal with. Then I stitched the main elephant outline and finally, the two inner legs and the little head cloth as three separate units. You may find a better order of stitching as you appliqué each elephant – the big advantage of repeating a motif several times is that you refine the strategies each time, so that you finish up with the quickest and most efficient route through.

Assembling the Quilt

1 From the fabric chosen for the narrow framing strips, cut two strips each 26in x 1½in (66cm x 3.8cm). Arrange the three rows of elephants in order and pin and stitch the two narrow strips between them (Fig 5a). Press seams towards the narrow strips, ironing from the front.

2 From the framing fabric cut four strips each 28in x 1½in (71.1cm x 3.8cm). Pin and stitch two of these to either side of the quilt (Fig 5b). Press the seams towards the narrow strips.

3 Pin and stitch the remaining two strips of framing fabric to the top and bottom of the quilt (Fig 5c). Press the seams towards the narrow strips as before.

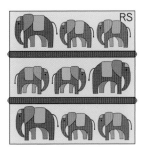

Fig 5a

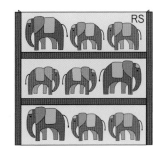

Fig 5b

Fig 5c

4 **Adding the final border:** From the fabric chosen for the final border (the same fabric that was used for the elephants' head cloths and saddle cloths) cut two strips each 30in x 2½in (76.2cm x 6.4cm). Pin and stitch these to either side of the quilt. Press the seams into the narrow framing strips. Cut two strips from the border fabric each 32in x 2½in (81.3cm x 6.4cm). Press the seams towards the narrow framing strips.

5 The final border has decorative strips of triangles appliquéd on to it. The top and bottom borders have three appliqué strips using the pattern in Fig 6, which has been reversed ready for tracing on to the fusible web (given at the end of the project). The reversed pattern for the longer appliqué is given full size in Fig 7 at the end of the project (enlarge it as described there). Because the side borders are slightly longer, a longer appliqué strip with seven triangles is used as the centre motif, with the shorter strips (with six triangles) from Fig 6 used on either side – see Fig 8.

Fig 8

6 Trace the design from Fig 6 on to the fusible web in the usual way ten times. Trace the design from Fig 7 on to the fusible web twice. Follow steps 2–3 at the start of the project to make the appliqué designs ready to position on the final border strips.

TIP

When removing the central areas of the fusible web in the design, I limited this to inside each triangle shape as shown in Fig 9 to keep the shape of the strip stable.

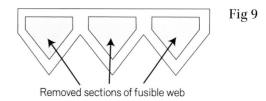

Fig 9

Removed sections of fusible web

7 Arrange three of the shorter triangle strips evenly along the top border. First, place one strip exactly in the middle of the border (match the centre of the border strip with the centre of the triangle strip) and then position the other two triangle strips on either side. The small gap between each strip will allow some flexibility in the arrangement. Iron the appliqué strips in place on the border strip in the usual way. Repeat this along the bottom border strip.

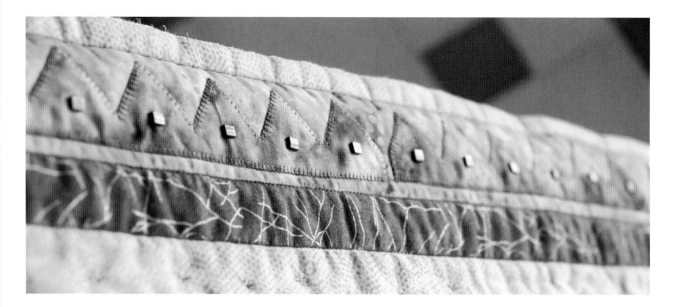

8 In the same way arrange three triangle strips on each of the side borders, placing the longer strip from Fig 7 exactly in the centre and the other two shorter triangle strips on either side. Iron into place. Now blanket stitch around the edges of all twelve triangle strips to complete the design.

Quilting and Finishing

9 Layer the quilt with wadding (batting) and backing fabric. Pin or tack (baste) the layers together ready for quilting either by hand or machine (see Quilting). I quilted by machine around the elephants close to the blanket stitching and also around the triangle strips, using the same thread for the quilting as was used for the machine blanket stitching. Extra machine quilting in the seams of the borders helped to keep everything in place. The background areas were left unquilted and instead I stitched stars at regular intervals across these areas to give some interest and control any puffiness in that area. The stars were made using a particular stitch on my machine that I am very fond of. Alternatively, they could be hand embroidered and would be equally effective. I added some very modern oblong beads to the stitched triangles to add more texture, plus sequins for the elephants' eyes and plaited variegated thread for their tails. Attach the tail with a few strong stitches so it swings loose from the design.

10 Finally, the quilt was bound in the same fabric as used in the background to the elephants – see Binding a Quilt.

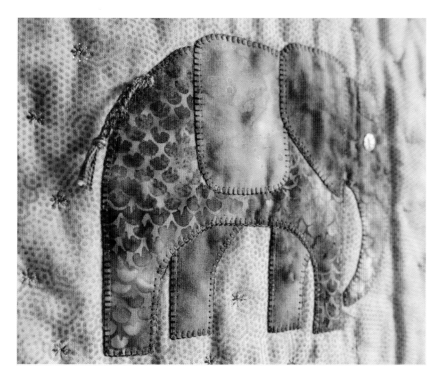

Patterns

Fig 1
Large Elephant Pattern – shown half size, so enlarge by 200% on a photocopier

Fig 2
Large Elephant Pattern Pieces (reversed design) – shown half size,
so enlarge by 200% on a photocopier
Dotted lines indicate where one appliqué piece fits under another
Arrows indicate direction of fabric grain

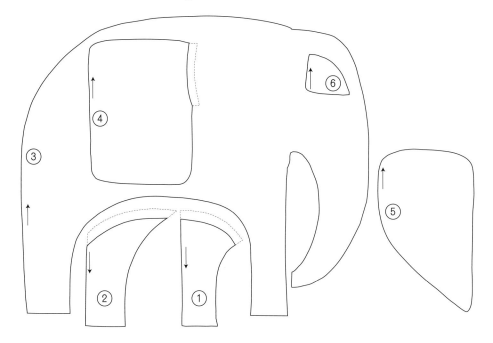

Fig 3
Small Elephant Pattern – shown half size, so
enlarge by 200% on a photocopier

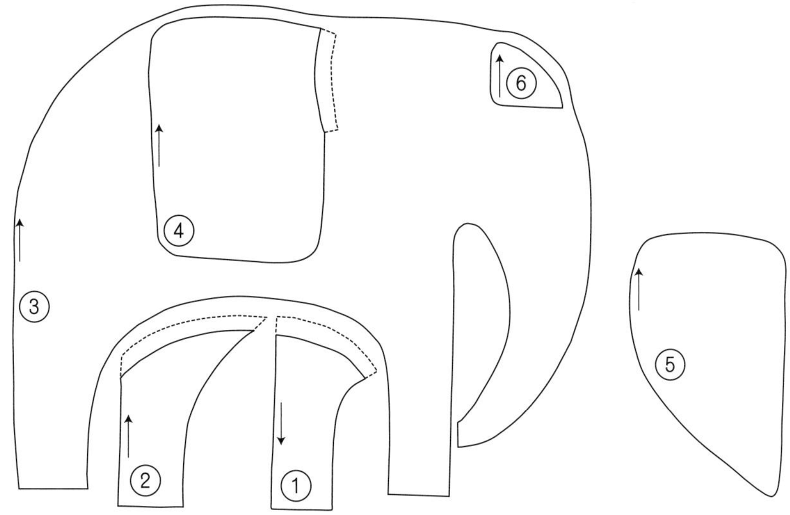

Fig 6
Triangles Pattern for Border – shown
half size, so enlarge by 200% on a photocopier

Fig 7
Triangles Pattern for Centre of Side Borders –
shown half size, so enlarge by
200% on a photocopier

Fig 4
Small Elephant Pattern Pieces (reversed design) –
shown half size, so enlarge by 200% on a photocopier
Dotted lines indicate where one appliqué piece fits under another
Arrows indicate direction of fabric grain

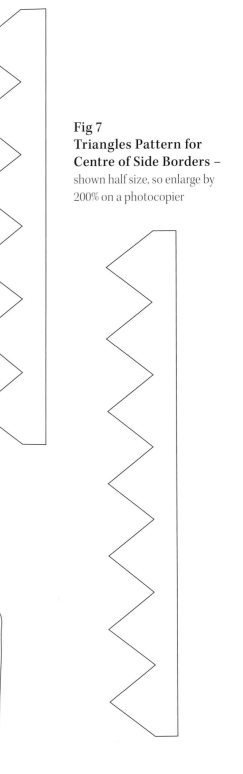

Baby Elephant Bag

Julia Reed took the baby elephant design from the Elephant Parade Wall Hanging and used it on a panel on each side of her small bag – an ideal gift for a little girl, or just to make and keep for yourself. The bag is a very simple shape and although lined it is quick and easy to make. The piece of background fabric for each elephant has a finished size of 7½in x 7in (19cm x 17.8cm), so any other appliqué design from this book or your own design could be used instead of the elephant to ring the changes for making other bags in the future. The long ties at the top of the bag add an interesting feature and keep the contents secure. Beads or buttons could be stitched on the ends of the ties as extra decoration if you wish.

Requirements

- Main bag fabric (excluding elephant panels on both sides) plus the handles ½yd/m

- Fabric to line bag 23in x 13in (58.4cm x 33cm)

- Wadding (batting) 23in x 13in (58.4cm x 33cm) and two strips each 1¼in x 26½in (3.2cm x 67.3cm)

- Two pieces of background fabric for the elephant blocks, each 8in x 7½in (20.3cm x 19.1cm)

- Fat eighth of batik fabric for the elephant

- Lighter batik fabric about 4in (10.2cm) square for two elephant ears (one for each block)

- Decorative fabric about 6in (15.2cm) square for two saddle cloths and two head cloths (one of each for each block)

- Yarn or thick thread for elephant tails

- Fusible web ¼yd/m (if using 17in/43.2cm wide type)

- Threads for blanket stitch

Size of finished block:

7½in x 7in (19cm x 17.8cm)

Size of finished bag:

10in (25.4cm) high x 12in (30.5cm) wide

TIP

If the design you want to use is too large to fit nicely on the background pieces, take it to a good photocopying shop together with the background block measurements and they will be able to reduce the design to fit. Take both the finished design and the accompanying set of reversed pieces so that both can be reduced at the same time ready to use. Alternatively, if you have a computer and scanner you could scan the images into your computer and reduce them as you print them.

Making the Elephant Blocks

Because the elephants are arranged by eye on each background piece of fabric, I would recommend using either a see-through appliqué pressing sheet or sheets of non-stick parchment baking paper when building up each elephant. Once completed, they can be removed from the paper or pressing sheet and placed as desired on the background fabric (see Tools for the Task: Fusible Web). Two blocks are needed, one for each side of the bag. Each finished block measures 7½in x 7in (19.1cm x 17.8cm).

1 From the elephant background fabric cut two squares each 8in x 7½in (20.3cm x 19.1cm).

2 Follow the instructions for Making a Small Elephant from the Elephant Parade Wall Hanging, starting with step 8 and then returning to steps 2–7 as advised. Use the pattern in Fig 3 and Fig 4, given at the end of the wall hanging instructions.

TIP

For the Elephant Parade Wall Hanging the second elephant fabric was used also for the elephants' legs, whereas for this bag project Julia used the second fabric only for the ears (see Requirements list).

3 Once the design is complete, carefully ease the elephant away from the pressing sheet or parchment paper. Make the second small elephant in the same way.

4 Position each elephant centrally on each 8in (20.3cm) wide x 7½in (19.1cm) high piece of background fabric. Press with a hot iron to fix the design to the fabric.

5 **Stitching the design:** Julia used a variegated thread to stitch around each elephant with machine blanket stitch (see Elephant Parade Wall Hanging, step 12), but of course the choice of hand or machine stitching is yours.

6 Add an eye either by stitching it or by using a fabric marker pen. Finally, make a tail from thick yarn or decorative thread – mine has a plaited tail. Attach it to the rear end of each elephant with a few strong stitches so that it swings loose from the design.

Constructing the Bag

7 From the main bag fabric cut the following pieces. Two strips 3in x 26½in (7.6cm x 67.3cm) for handles. One strip 2in x 24½in (5.1cm x 62.2cm) for the top lining strip. This strip may be joined if necessary. Four pieces each 7½in x 2¾in (19.1cm x 7cm) for the side pieces (call these A). One piece 12½in x 5in (31.8cm x 12.7cm) for the base of the bag (call this B). Two strips each 2¼in x 12½in (5.7cm x 31.8cm) for the top section of the bag (call these C). Two strips each 1¼in x 9½in (3.2cm x 24.1cm) for ties.

8 Take the four pieces (A) and pin and stitch a strip to either side of both elephant blocks (Fig 5). Press seams away from the blocks, ironing from the front.

Fig 5

9 Take piece (B) and pin and stitch an elephant block to each of the longer sides of piece (B) as in Fig 6. Press the seams away from the elephant blocks, ironing from the front.

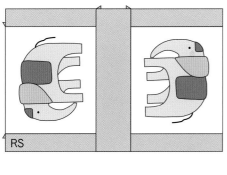

Fig 6

TIP

Note that the elephants are both arranged with their feet towards the centre strip of the bag as in Fig 6. If you place them with their heads towards the centre, the final bag will have upside-down elephants!

10 Pin and stitch the two strips (C) to either end of the elephant blocks as in Fig 7. Press the seams away from the elephant blocks.

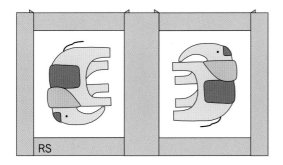

Fig 7

11 Cut a piece of lining fabric and a piece of wadding (batting) both 23in x 13in (58.4cm x 33cm). Place the lining fabric down on a surface with right side *downwards*. Place the wadding on to it and finally the elephant rectangle with right side *upwards*. The edges of the wadding and lining should be level with each other and show all around the edges of the bag rectangle. Pin or tack (baste) the layers together ready for quilting.

12 **Quilting the design:** Use a marking pencil or hera to mark across the centre of the base of the bag, that is, the centre rectangle (B), from top to bottom (Fig 8a). Machine quilt this line and then three lines on either side of it at ⅜in (1cm) intervals, making seven lines altogether (Fig 8b). This forms the base of the bag. Quilt around the elephants by hand or machine and also in the seams of the border strips.

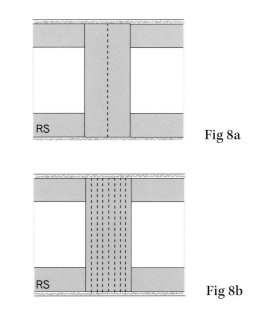

Fig 8a

Fig 8b

Assembling the Bag

1 Trim the quilted layers to 22½in x 12½in (57.2cm x 31.8cm). Fold the rectangle in half across the quilted base with right sides together. Make a mark a generous ¼in (6mm) from either side on the top edge and ¾in (1.9cm) from either side at the bottom folded edge. Join these points with a marking pencil to show the seam line (Fig 9). Pin together and stitch along the drawn lines firmly through all the layers.

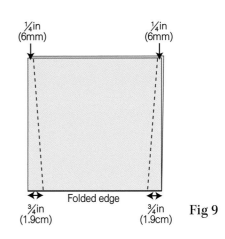

Fig 9

2 Trim the seams to a ¼in (6mm) seam allowance. Either zigzag the raw edges by machine to neaten them or bind them with a folded strip of lining fabric.

3 Still keeping the bag wrong side outwards, match the side seams at the top of the bag and flatten the bottom to make a triangular shape (Fig 10). Mark a line across each of the two quilted triangular points 1¼in (3.2cm) from the corner and stitch through all layers (Fig 11). This creates a flat base to the bag. Trim each triangular stitched corner ¼in (6mm) beyond the stitching. Neaten the raw edges of the seams as before.

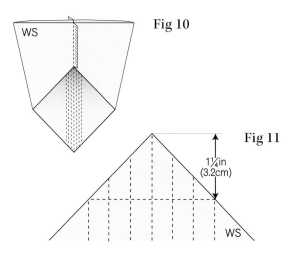

Fig 10

WS

1¼in (3.2cm)

Fig 11

WS

4 **Making the handles:** Take the two 3in x 26½in (7.6cm x 67.3cm) handle strips cut earlier. Cut two strips of wadding each 1¼in x 26½in (3.2cm x 67.3cm).

5 Press over a ¼in (6mm) turning to the wrong side on both long sides of both strips of fabric. Lay a strip of wadding on the wrong side of each fabric strip, tucking it under one long folded edge as in Fig 12a. Fold each fabric strip in half with wrong sides together to enclose the wadding, matching the folded edges of the fabric. Press and pin in position. Topstitch the outer edges of each strip and also down the centre (Fig 12b).

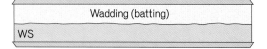

Wadding (batting)

WS

Fig 12a

Raw ends

RS

Raw ends

Fig 12b

6 **Making the ties:** Take the two 1¼in x 9½in (3.2cm x 24.1cm) tie strips cut earlier and press over a ¼in (6mm) turning on each of the long sides and on one of the short sides. Fold each strip in half lengthwise with wrong sides facing and press. Topstitch along each folded side.

7 **Finishing the bag top:** Pin the raw end of each tie to the outside of the top edge of the bag, right sides facing, positioning each tie exactly midway between the two side seams and matching the raw edges. Position and pin each end of one handle as in Fig 13. The ends of the handle should be 2¼in (5.7cm) from the pinned tie on either side. Repeat this with the second handle on either side of the other tie strip.

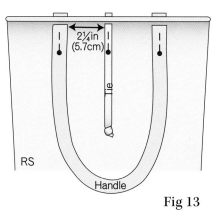

2¼in (5.7cm)

Tie

RS

Handle

Fig 13

8 Take the 2in x 24½in (5.1cm x 62.2cm) strip cut earlier for the top lining and stitch the short sides together to make a circle.

9 Pin the strip to the outside of the top edge of the bag, right sides facing. Stitch along the top edge, stitching through all the layers of the bag and the handles and ties.

TIP

If you find your top lining circle does not fit the top edge of the bag exactly, don't worry – just adjust the seam in the lining circle until it fits the bag nicely.

10 Fold the lining strip over to the inside of the bag along the stitched seam. Finger-press a ¼in (6mm) turning on the bottom edge of the lining strip and pin this edge in place on the lining of the bag. Slipstitch it into place by hand.

11 Finally, topstitch along the top edge of the bag to give a firm finish. Make a firm knot at the end of each tie or stitch on a decorative bead to add interest if you desire.

Pansy Baskets

Like most of my quilts, this Pansy Basket started with a collection of fabrics, in this case some amazing Kaffe Fassett striped fabrics that I wanted to use but was reluctant to cut up too much, as the different widths of the stripes was an integral part of their attraction. They reminded me of the Madras cotton bedspreads that we all had in the sixties – I remember my first dressmaking attempt using my grandmother's hand sewing machine was a shift dress made from one of these bedspreads. It seated and creased every time I moved or sat down but I thought it was wonderful and I still love that woven textured look.

There was a range of two-tone shot plain cottons that complemented the stripes wonderfully and despite the loose weave I could not resist using them for this blanket stitch quilt. The background fabric was a firmer charcoal-coloured cotton which helped to stabilize the appliqué pieces and the bonus was that I was able to use thicker thread to blanket stitch by hand around the pieces, as the loose weave made it easier to pull the thread through the fabric.

There are dozens of appliqué basket designs to be found in traditional quilts, many complex and containing a selection of flowers and leaves. I needed to use a basket that would showcase my striped fabrics, so I chose one with a simple wide outline and central handle, much like the basket that stands on the floor in our kitchen to hold fresh vegetables. The plain fabrics I had chosen were mainly mauves and pinks, so I felt that the flowers in my basket just had to be pansies. I wanted to arrange the baskets in rows, as if they were all displayed on the shelves of an open kitchen dresser, to continue the country feel of the quilt design.

Pansy Baskets Quilt

For this quilt, the baskets are made as individual appliqué blocks, which are then joined into horizontal rows and combined to make the quilt. Narrow borders of stripes edge the centre design, plus a pieced border of squares on point, which is based on a Seminole patchwork design and uses up the left-overs from the striped fabrics. The shelves that the baskets stand on are defined by rows of decorative stitch patterns made by my sewing machine using a thicker thread. I love to mix hand work and machine stitching in a quilt as it can add richness and variety to the design.

There are eighteen pansy basket blocks in the quilt and I used six different striped fabrics for the baskets, making three baskets from each fabric. For the pansies I collected as many pink/mauve fabrics that I could find and used them in different combinations for each basket of flowers. For the leaves one green fabric was used throughout. Both borders were cut from the same striped fabric used in the baskets. For the binding I used a fabric that was from the range I had collected but had not used in the quilt itself as yet. It was a new addition but one that fitted in well with the collection.

Requirements

- A fat quarter each of six different striped fabrics for the baskets and border squares

- Assorted pink/mauve fabrics for the pansies ¾yd/0.75m in total

- A fat quarter of a green fabric for leaves

- Background fabric 2yd/m

- Additional striped fabric for borders (as used in the baskets) ½yd/m

- Wadding (batting) 53in (134.6cm) square

- Backing fabric 53in (134.6cm) square

- Binding fabric ½yd/m

- Fusible web 2yd/m (if using 17in/43.2cm wide)

- Threads for blanket stitch

Size of finished block:

10½in x 8½in (26.7cm x 21.6cm)

Size of finished quilt:

50in x 50½in (127cm x 128.3cm)

TIP

Because this is quite a complex appliqué design, I would strongly recommend using either a see-through appliqué pressing sheet or sheets of non-stick parchment baking paper when building up each appliqué basket – see Tools for the Task.

Making a Pansy Basket Block

1 Each pansy basket block needs background fabric measuring 11in x 9in (27.9cm x 22.9cm). For this quilt you will need eighteen pieces of background fabric this size, one for each block, plus four pieces of background fabric each 9in x 5¾in (22.9cm x 14.6cm) to be used later when assembling the completed blocks. You could cut all the background rectangles at this stage ready to use, or cut each piece as you need it.

2 **Choosing the fabrics:** Use the patterns given full size at the end of the project instructions. The finished design of the basket with four pansies and four leaves is given in Fig 1. Each pansy is made of two pieces, using two different fabrics, with the darker fabric usually for the lower part of the flower. Three of the pansies are made from the same pattern pieces (pieces 7 and 8 in Fig 2) and the fourth is slightly larger, using pattern pieces 9 and 10 in Fig 2. To keep the design simple, I used the same two fabrics for the outer two pansies and a different pair for the two inner flowers that overlap the handle. The photograph here of one basket may help you choose from your own selection, although you could limit the fabrics to just two per basket, or make each flower different. For the leaves I used one fabric throughout – use more if you would like to.

3 **Tracing the design:** When using fusible web the design must be reversed. Fig 2 gives each reversed shape to make the pansy basket design. The dashed lines should be included – they indicate areas where one shape is overlapped by another. Place the fusible web smooth side *uppermost* over the ten shapes in Fig 2. Note that shapes 7 and 8 need to be traced on to the fusible web three times each to make the three smaller pansies in the design. Follow the instructions given in Essential Techniques: Using Fusible Web for tracing and cutting out the required shapes from the fusible web. Remove the inner section of fusible web from every piece except leaf 4, which is too small and fiddly. When the inner area is cut from piece 2, the basket handle (piece 1), which is drawn in this area, can now be cut out in the same way.

4 Take the fabrics chosen for the design. Place each cut piece of fusible web with the rough side *downwards* on the *wrong* side of each chosen fabric, matching the grain line arrow with the grain or weave of the fabric. Follow the instructions given in Essential Techniques: Using Fusible Web to iron the fusible web in place and to cut out each piece of the design.

5 **Building up the design:** You will need to work on an ironing surface to position each piece, so at this stage trace the whole design from Fig 1 clearly on to thin paper or tracing paper – alternatively, photocopy it to save time and energy. Cut a piece of non-stick parchment baking paper a little larger than the finished design in Fig 1, or use a see-through appliqué pressing sheet.

6 Place the paper or pressing sheet over your copy of Fig 1 on the ironing surface. Fix both layers in place on the ironing surface with pins or masking tape at the corners. Starting with piece 1 (the basket handle), remove the paper backing. Position the handle right side *up*, glue side *down* in the correct place on the parchment paper or pressing sheet. Press lightly with the iron to stick it on to the parchment paper or pressing sheet. Alternatively, you can arrange the entire design and make any final adjustments before ironing anything. A final pressing of the whole piece will fix the design in place on the paper or pressing sheet. Now place piece 2 (the basket) into position and iron that in place.

7 Arrange the four leaves (pieces 3, 4, 5 and 6) in position, using the drawing of Fig 1 beneath to make sure they overlap the basket a little. Iron in place.

8 Position the two sections of each of the three smaller pansies (each made up of pieces 7 and 8). Place the larger piece 7 first, then the smaller piece 8, which overlaps it slightly (Fig 3). Iron in place. Draw on to each pansy the extra petal lines, as shown in Fig 4.

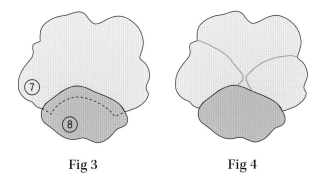

Fig 3   Fig 4

9 Repeat this process with the large pansy, using pieces 9 and 10 and drawing on the extra petal lines, using the original drawing of Fig 1 as a guide.

10 **Stitching the design:** I stitched the design by hand, using a slightly thicker thread than usual, but if you wish to machine stitch it, that will be fine. I often use Gütermann silk thread for hand blanket stitch appliqué but for this design I chose YLI Jeans Stitch, and a fine sewing needle (crewel embroidery 8 or 9). Black thread is often used to outline this type of design, but any thread colour will be fine. I used a mauve for the basket and a variegated mauve thread for the pansies. For the leaves I used a matching thread. See Tools for the Task: Threads and Needles for more information on your choices. For blanket stitching refer to Essential Techniques: Blanket Stitching by Hand or Blanket Stitching by Machine. I stitched around the basket and the handle first, then the leaves and finally the pansies, working from the top petal downwards to the bottom of each flower. You may prefer a different order of stitching, which is fine.

11 I often cut away the back layers after blanket stitching to reduce the thicknesses for quilting but on this occasion I felt the loose weave of the appliqué fabrics would be stabilized by leaving all the layers intact.

12 Finally, fill in the centre of each pansy with stitches to bring the flower to life.

Making More Blocks

13 Making the first block always takes a long time: trying out stitches and threads, choosing fabrics, mastering the nuances of the design and so on. Once this block is completed, it becomes your reference for all those decisions made as you worked on it, and making the others becomes far easier. Always keep the finished blocks in view as you select the fabrics for the next pansy basket as this will give an overview of the growing collection of blocks and ensure that the colours are evenly distributed in the quilt. For my quilt I made eighteen pansy baskets, but you might like to make a smaller design with just seven blocks as shown in Fig 5 or even just one block for the centre of a cushion or bag.

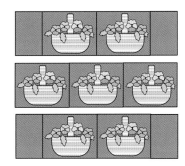

Fig 5

Assembling the Quilt

1 Arrange the blocks into rows as Fig 6a. Because the rows are offset there will be a space at either end of rows 2 and 4. This is where the extra rectangles of background fabric are needed. If you have not yet cut the four rectangles, all 9in x 5¾in (22.9cm x 14.6cm), do so now. Place each rectangle in position (Fig 6b).

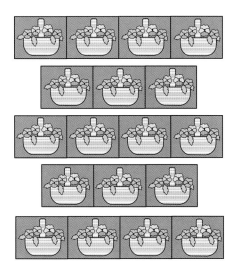

Fig 6a

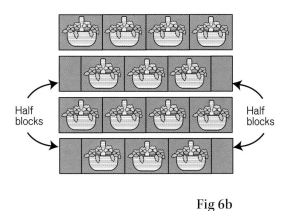

Half
blocks

Half
blocks

Fig 6b

2 Stitch the blocks into five rows as Fig 6b. Press seams to one side, ironing from the front. With this offset arrangement, the seams of the blocks in each row do not have to be matched with those of the next row, so they can be pressed to whichever side you wish.

3 Pin and stitch the five rows together to make the centre of the quilt. Press seams to one side.

Adding the Borders

4 Measure the quilt across its centre in both directions. It should be 43½in (110.5cm) from side to side and 43in (109.2cm) from top to bottom. If not, don't worry, just use your own measurements for the length of the border strips and that will be fine.

5 **Adding the inner strip border:** From the fabric for the first narrow border around the centre design cut two strips each 1¼in (3.2cm) wide and 43in (109.2cm) long (or measurement to match your quilt depth).Pin and stitch to either side of the quilt. Press seams outwards.

6 Measure across the centre of the quilt. It should now measure 45in (114.3cm). From the same fabric cut two strips 1¼in (3.2cm) wide and 45in (114.3cm) long (or length to match your quilt measurement). Pin and stitch these strips to the top and bottom of the quilt. Press the seams outwards, away from the quilt.

7 **Adding the squares-on-point border:** This is made up of squares of assorted fabrics used for the baskets, which are placed on point and edged with triangles of the background fabric, as in Fig 7.

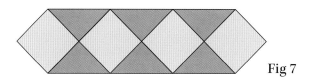

Fig 7

8 From the fabrics used for the baskets cut eighty-four squares each 2in x 2in (5.1 x 5.1cm). From the background fabric cut eighty-four squares each 2⅜in x 2⅜in (6cm x 6cm). Cut each square of background fabric in half diagonally to give 168 half-square triangles.

9 Pin and stitch a triangle of background fabric to the opposite sides of each of the squares (Fig 8).

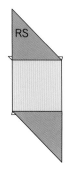

RS

Fig 8

10 Pin and stitch two pieced units together, stepping the second piece down as in Fig 9 and matching seams carefully. Press the seam to one side.

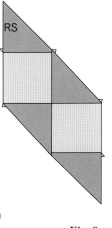

11 Join twenty-nine pieces together in this way to make the border strip for one side. Repeat this a total of four times to make the border strips for the each side of the quilt.

Fig 9

TIP

The quilt is not an exact square, but there is so little difference between the length and the width that this border can be safely made from four pieces with the same number of squares on point and then tweaked and stretched slightly to fit each quilt side. Amazing what an iron can do...

12 An extra, different unit is needed on one end of each strip to make the four corners fit together. To the remaining four 2in (5.1cm) squares, pin and stitch two background triangles as shown in Fig 10. Stitch these on to one end of each strip (Fig 11).

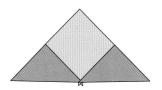

Fig 10

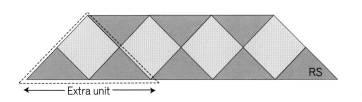

Extra unit

RS

Fig 11

13 Mark the turning corner of the seam line at each corner of the quilt with a pencilled dot on the wrong side (Fig 12a). Do the same at either end of each border strip (Fig 12b).

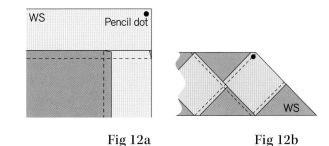

WS   Pencil dot

WS

Fig 12a   **Fig 12b**

14 Pin each border strip to the sides of the quilt, matching corner dots. It needs to fit *exactly*, so if it doesn't adjust the borders to fit the quilt. If the border strip is too long, re-stitch a few seams that join the pieced units with a slightly wider seam allowance until it fits. If the border is too short, press it with the iron stretching it slightly until it fits the quilt. Once the border lengths are correct, pin and stitch them to the quilt, starting and finishing exactly at the marked dots each time.

15 Finally, pin and stitch the corner diagonal seams, matching the seams carefully (Fig 13). Press these four seams open to help the mitred corners to lie flat.

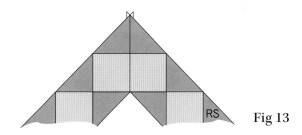

RS   **Fig 13**

16 **Adding the outer border:** Measure the quilt from top to bottom, down the centre. Cut two strips of border fabric, each 1½in (3.8cm) wide and a length to match the quilt. Pin and stitch these to either side of the quilt. Press seams outwards, away from the quilt.

17 Measure across the centre of the quilt. From the same fabric cut two strips 1½in (3.8cm) wide and in a length to match the quilt width. Pin and stitch these to the top and bottom of the quilt. Press seams outwards.

Quilting and Finishing

18 Layer the quilt with wadding (batting) and backing fabric – see Quilting. I quilted in the baskets and outlined the pansies and baskets by hand. I then used a decorative stitch of tiny leaves to quilt vertical lines on the background fabric 2in (5cm) apart. As these were stitched with thread to match the charcoal background, they add interest and texture without detracting from the baskets. The shelves were created by two parallel lines of straight stitching with a broad decorative stitch between them, all in a thicker thread in a contrasting bright pink colour.

19 For the double-fold binding I used a fabric not used in the quilt itself but which fitted in well. I used a starting width of 2½in – see Binding a Quilt.

Michelle Clark used the pansy block in her bed quilt placed on point on a dark outer square. She also took the pansies and created a small nosegay to use in blocks alongside the large basket design. The pattern for this is shown full size in Fig 14 at the end of this chapter and uses the larger pansy (pieces 9 and 10 in Fig 2) and the large leaf piece 5, also from Fig 2. Each flower and leaf is used four times to make the design.

Patterns

Fig 1
Pattern – shown full size

Fig 2
Pattern Pieces (reversed design) – shown full size
Dotted lines indicate where one appliqué piece fits under another
Arrows indicate fabric grain

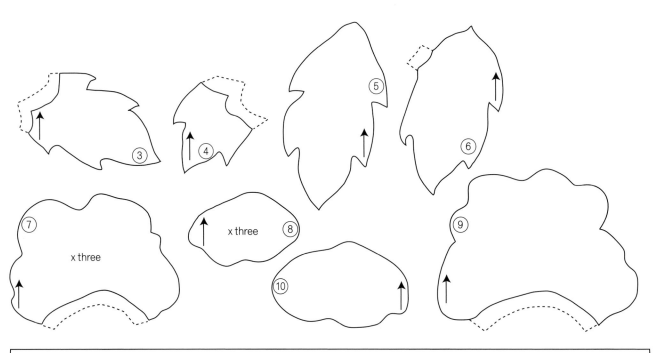

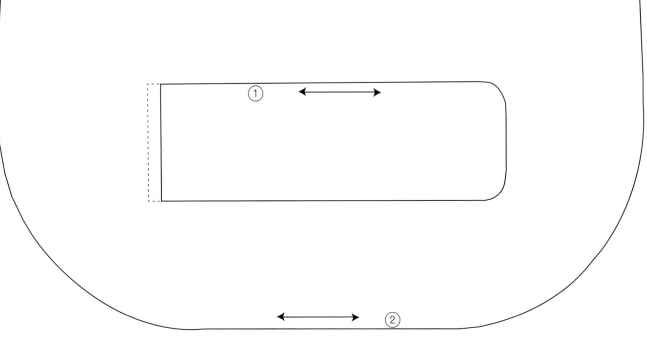

Fig 14
Pattern for Michele Clarke's alternate pansy quilt –
shown full size

Vintage Butterflies

I saw this butterfly design on an antique quilt in a magazine years ago and fell in love with it. Each butterfly was pieced (not appliquéd), using dozens of fabrics from the 1920s–30s, with traditional calico as the background fabric. Sometime later I found a pattern for the pieced block, so all I needed was the fabric. At this time I was travelling and teaching in America quite regularly, and so added to my collection of pretty prints and accompanying plains. Finally, in Florida, I bought the huge amount of cream fabric for the background and backing. And I do mean a huge amount, as a double quilt takes a total of at least eight yards or metres of fabric, with a similar amount for the backing.

Before embarking on the quilt itself, I decided to try out the design with some hand-dyed fabric to give it a very different look. It only took the making of one block to show me that I didn't enjoy hand-piecing as much as I thought I did. I made four blocks before admitting that it was not what I wanted to do for the next year! By then I had become addicted to hand blanket stitch appliqué, so was able to adapt the design as an appliqué which could be stuck into place on a background square and outlined in blanket stitch – bliss! From then on there was no stopping me: each block was cut and assembled quickly using fusible web around the edges of each piece. How fortunate that I had bought so much of that cream fabric – by the time I had made each block and added the pieced scrappy border, there was only just enough left for the back of the quilt with not a scrap to spare.

The second project in this chapter uses a smaller and less complex butterfly for a summery table runner and matching napkins. Today's designer fabrics give a very different and modern look to the butterfly design and make a lovely table set.

Butterfly Quilt

I made a double bed-size quilt but the butterfly block could be used in smaller projects, such as a cushion made from one block or a cot quilt with twelve butterflies (3 x 4 blocks). The complex Seminole border could be replaced with simple frames to complete the design if you prefer.

My quilt has a centre area of thirty-five butterfly blocks framed on three sides by a narrow scrap border of squares on point. Beyond this I added another row of butterfly blocks, twenty-one in total, and finished with a wider Seminole border of squares on all four sides. You may prefer to limit the butterfly blocks to that centre 5 x 7 blocks and simply frame that with a series of straight frames. For hand blanket stitch I like to use Gütermann silk thread and normal cotton machine thread for machine blanket stitch. If making a quilt specifically for a bed, it can work well to limit the wide border design to the sides and bottom edge of the quilt, with just the final border added on all four sides. This helps to centre the main design on the bed, plus has the bonus of showing immediately which way round the quilt needs to go...

Requirements

- Background fabric 6½yd (6m)
- Assorted fabrics for butterflies, borders and binding (as many as possible) 4yd (3½m) in total
- Fusible web about 4sq yd (3½sq m) for the whole quilt
- Backing fabric 7yd (6½m) of 42in–44in (107cm–112cm) wide
- Wadding (batting) 98in x 90in (249cm x 229cm)
- Threads for the blanket stitch and butterfly antennae

Size of finished block:

10in x 10in (25.4cm x 25.4cm)

Size of finished quilt:

94in x 86½in (239cm x 220cm)

TIP

Because this is quite a complex design, I would strongly recommend using either a see-through appliqué pressing sheet or sheets of non-stick parchment baking paper when building up each basket (see Tools for the Task). It is also advisable to buy fusible web as you need it a yard or metre at a time as it can deteriorate if stored too long.

Making a Butterfly Block

The appliqué pieces are stuck in place with a narrow strip of fusible web such as Bondaweb before edging with blanket stitch, either by hand or by machine. Every butterfly uses six different fabrics for the wings, or fewer if preferred, plus an extra fabric for the body. Each of the butterflies in my own quilt used a different set of fabrics, making it an ideal design for a scrap quilt.

Use the photograph of one butterfly plus the outlines given in Figs 1a and 1b (given at the end of the project) to choose the fabrics for the first block. Enlarge the patterns as described. These two halves will be traced and joined to make a master copy later. The pieces in the right wing are numbered 1–6, while their opposites in the left wing are numbered 1R–6R (R = reversed: each piece for the right-hand wing is drawn in reversed form for the left-hand wing).

1 From the background fabric cut a square measuring 10½in x 10½in (26.7cm x 26.7cm). Fold the square lightly into four diagonally. The fold lines will be used as a guide for positioning the butterfly design on point on the background square. The dotted lines in the traced design should match the fold lines in the square of fabric.

2 When using a fusible web the design must be reversed. Fig 2 (at the end of the project) gives each reversed shape to make the butterfly design. Place the fusible web smooth side *uppermost* over the thirteen shapes in Fig 2. Trace each section including any dotted areas. Follow the general instructions for tracing and cutting out the required shapes from the fusible web in Essential Techniques: Using Fusible Web.

3 Carefully cut out the central area of fusible web from each piece and remove it, leaving only about ⅛in (3mm) inside the drawn line (Fig 3). The removed pieces of fusible can be kept for later projects.

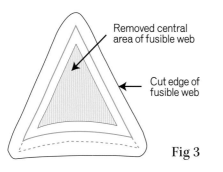

Removed central area of fusible web

Cut edge of fusible web

Fig 3

4 Select six fabrics for the butterfly wings and one for the body. Place each cut piece of fusible web with the rough side *downwards* on the *wrong* side of each chosen fabric, matching the grain line arrow with the grain or weave of the fabric. Press with an iron to stick the fusible web to the fabric.

5 Now cut accurately along the drawn line through both paper and fabric. Include in the cut-out shape any dotted area (Fig 4).

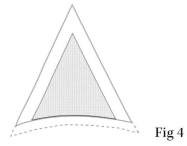

Fig 4

6 **Building up the design:** You will need to work on an ironing surface to position each piece, so make a master copy of the butterfly from the two half shapes in Fig 1a and 1b (enlarged as described). Trace each half of the design from Fig 1a and Fig 1b clearly on to thin paper or tracing paper (or photocopy them). Match the two traced sections together along the dotted line and stick them together to make the complete butterfly. Cut non-stick parchment paper a little larger than the finished design or use a see-through appliqué pressing sheet.

7 If you are using an appliqué pressing sheet, lay it over the master copy – you will be able to see the design through the plastic sheet. The non-stick baking parchment paper is less transparent but still should allow the design to show through well enough for positioning the pieces on to it. The whole butterfly design will be assembled and ironed on to the pressing sheet or parchment paper. Once it is complete, only then will it be carefully peeled away from the background plastic or paper and then re-positioned and ironed in place on the background fabric. Arrange the cut shapes on the pressing sheet or parchment paper (*not* on the background fabric), right side *up*, glue side *down*, using the underlying drawn butterfly as a guide for positioning each piece.

8 Starting with pieces 1 and 1R (the right wing-point and the matching reversed left wing-point) remove the paper backing. Position the two shapes right side *up*, glue side *down* in the correct place on the pressing sheet or parchment paper. Iron them on to the pressing sheet or parchment paper to stick them down.

9 Place pieces 2 and 2R in position and iron into place. Arrange pieces 3, 4 and 5, 3R, 4R and 5R in position, making sure they overlap and fit together with a smooth outline before fixing them with the iron. Position pieces 6 and 6R and iron in place. Finally, add the butterfly body, piece 7, and iron it on to complete the design.

10 Now carefully ease the butterfly away from the pressing sheet or parchment paper.

11 Place the cut square of background fabric on to the drawing of the butterfly in Fig 1a with right side upwards. Line up the folded diagonal lines on the fabric with the dotted diagonal lines marked on Fig 1a. Position the fabric butterfly on the background fabric using the drawn outlines from Fig 1a as a guide. Press with the iron to fix the butterfly on the background fabric.

12 Finally, trace the lines of the antennae on to the background fabric with a fine marking pencil.

13 **Stitching the design:** I stitched the design by hand, using a slightly thicker thread than usual (a Gütermann silk thread) and a fine sewing needle, such as a Sharps 9 or 10. Black is often used to outline this type of design but any colour will be fine. See the Tools for the Task: Threads and Needles for more information. For information on blanket stitching, refer to Essential Techniques: Blanket Stitching by Hand or Blanket Stitching by Machine.

14 After stitching the edges of the butterfly, the layers may be reduced by turning the whole piece over and cutting away the background areas within the blanket-stitched edges ¼in (6mm) away from the stitching. This is not obligatory, especially with a complex design like this one where the background fabric helps to keep the design stable, so if your nerve fails you, just leave all the layers intact.

15 Finally, stitch the butterfly's antennae, using the same thread as that used for the edging blanket stitch. Either backstitch or stem stitch is effective as both make a solid line of stitching.

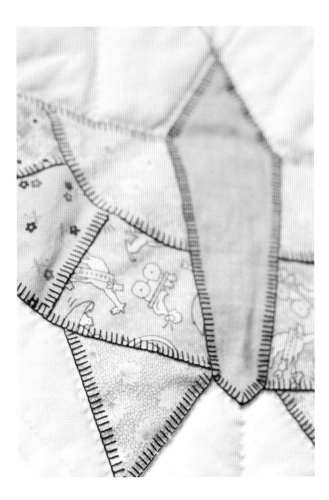

Assembling the Quilt

The main central part of the design is made from thirty-five of the butterfly blocks, joined into seven rows each containing five blocks (Fig 5). Arrange the butterflies as shown. There should be seven rows of butterfly blocks with five butterfly blocks in each horizontal row.

Fig 5

1 Pin and stitch the top row of blocks together. Press the seams to one side, ironing from the front of the work.

2 Pin and stitch the second row of blocks together. Press the seams in the opposite direction to row 1, ironing from the front of the work. Continue to pin and stitch each row, pressing seams in alternate directions to help lock them.

3 Join the rows together, matching seams carefully. Press seams to one side from the front.

4 Cut two strips of background fabric each 1½in (3.8cm) wide and in a length to fit the sides of the quilt (this should be 70½in/179.1cm but if your quilt has different measurements just cut the strips to match your own quilt). Pin and stitch the two side strips on to the quilt. Press the seams away from the quilt.

5 Measure across the quilt from side to side. Cut two more strips of background fabric (1½in/3.8cm) wide) and in this length (this should be 52½in/133.4cm but if your quilt measures a different amount, do as before and cut the length to match your quilt). Pin and stitch the top and bottom strips to the quilt. Press the seams outwards, away from the quilt.

Making the Inner Border

The first inner border of the quilt runs along both sides and across the bottom but not the top of the quilt. Based on the Seminole patchwork design, it is made up of squares of assorted fabrics used for the butterflies, which are placed on point and edged with triangles of the background fabric as in Fig 6.

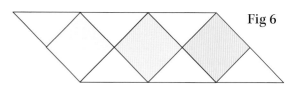

Fig 6

6 From the fabrics used for the butterflies cut ninety-six squares each 2¼in x 2¼in (5.7cm x 5.7cm). From the background fabric cut 101 squares each 2⅝in x 2⅝in (6.7cm x 6.7cm). Cut each square of background fabric in half diagonally to give 202 half-square triangles.

7 Pin and stitch a triangle of background fabric to opposite sides of each of the squares (Fig 7).

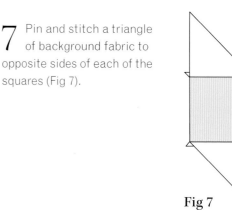

RS

Fig 7

8 Pin and stitch the two pieced units together, stepping the second piece down as in Fig 8 and matching the seams carefully. Press the seam to one side.

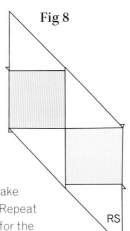

Fig 8

9 Join twenty-nine pieces together in this way to make the border strip for one side. Repeat this to make the border strip for the opposite side of the quilt. To square the ends of the border strips, add a cut triangle of background fabric to either end (Fig 9a). Trim the ends to straighten the border strip ¼in (6mm) beyond the corner of the square on point (Fig 9b).

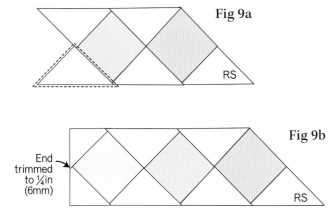

Fig 9a

RS

End trimmed to ¼in (6mm)

Fig 9b

RS

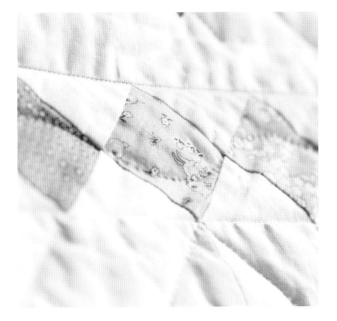

10 Pin and stitch each side border strip to the quilt. Press the seams outwards, away from the quilt.

TIP

If the border is too short or too long, you can add more pieced units or remove some to make it fit your quilt. If it is only slightly too small, press the border strip with the iron, stretching it slightly until it fits the quilt exactly.

11 For the sides of the quilt arrange two rows each of seven butterfly blocks (Fig 10a). Pin and stitch them together.

12 Cut four strips of background fabric each 1½in x 10½in (3.8cm x 26.7cm). Pin and stitch a strip to either end of the butterfly border strips (Fig 10b).

Fig 10a

Fig 10b

13 Join the butterfly border strips to the sides of the quilt, matching seams carefully. Press the seams away from the main quilt.

14 To make the bottom border, make a border strip of thirty squares on point as in steps 7–9. Also make two short strips with four squares on point. Straighten both ends of each strip as in step 9.

15 Pin and stitch the long border strip to the bottom edge of the quilt. Press the seams outwards away from the quilt.

16 Cut two strips of background fabric each 1½in x 10½in (3.8cm x 26.7cm). Arrange the remaining seven butterfly blocks in a strip, together with the two narrow strips of background fabric and also the two short strips of squares on point as in Fig 11. Pin and stitch them together.

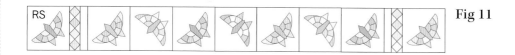

Fig 11

17 Join this butterfly border strip to the bottom edge of the quilt, matching seams carefully.

Making the Outer Border

This final Seminole border will certainly use up much of your left-over fabric from the butterflies, but if you prefer just add a simple framing border from strips cut 5in (12.7cm) wide.

18 To make the Seminole border, from the fabrics used for the butterflies cut 414 squares each 2¼in x 2¼in (5.7cm x 5.7cm). From the background fabric cut 138 squares each 2⅝in x 2⅝in (6.7cm x 6.7cm). Cut each square of background fabric in half diagonally to give 276 half-square triangles.

19 Stitch the squares into rows of three, with a triangle of background fabric at either end as in Fig 12a. Make 130 of these. Leave the remaining squares and triangles until later.

20 Pin and stitch two pieced units together, stepping the second piece down as in Fig 12b and matching the seams carefully. Press the seam to one side.

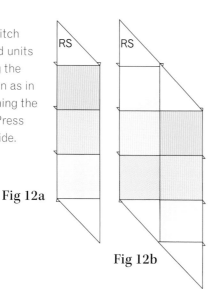

Fig 12a

Fig 12b

21 Join thirty-four pieced units together in this way to make the strips for one side. Make a second strip this length for the other side of the quilt. Make two strips each with thirty-one pieced units for the top and bottom of the quilt.

22 An extra, different unit is needed on one end of each strip to make the four corners fit together. Stitch four pieced units as in Fig 13a. Stitch the four units together to make the large pieced triangle in Fig 13b. Make four of these large pieced triangles.

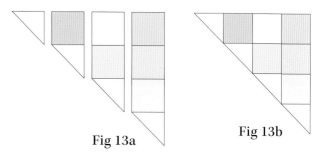

Fig 13a

Fig 13b

23 Pin and stitch a pieced triangle to one end of each border strip (Fig 14).

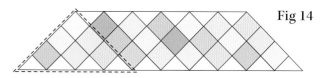

Fig 14

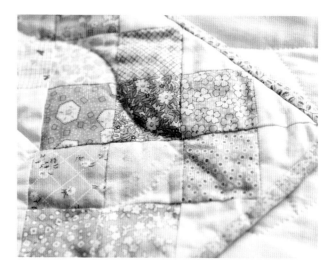

24 Mark the turning corner of the seam line at each of the four corners of the main quilt with a pencilled dot on the wrong side (Fig 15a). Do the same at either end of each border strip (Fig 15b).

WS

Fig 15a

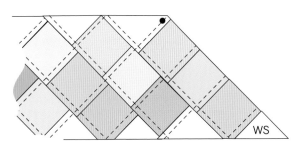

WS

Fig 15b

25 Pin each border strip to the sides of the quilt, matching the corner dots. Stitch the strips in place, starting and finishing exactly at the marked dots each time.

26 Finally, pin and stitch the corner diagonal seams, matching the seams carefully (Fig 16). Press these four seams open to help the mitred corners to lie flat.

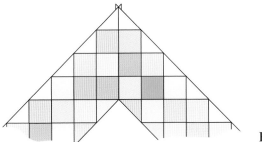

Fig 16

Quilting and Finishing

As this was an heirloom project that I planned to be the summer quilt for our bed, I was happy to spend the time (and get the pleasure) quilting it by hand. I kept the quilting quite simple and not too dense so that it did not overshadow the appliqué design, quilting around each butterfly and then diagonally in lines across the background of each block. The borders of squares on point were quilted in curves through the centres of each square – simple but enough to hold the pieces in place, which is what quilting is for, after all (see Fig 17a and 17b). Once quilted, the edges of the quilt were bound with joined strips of assorted butterfly fabrics – see Binding a Quilt.

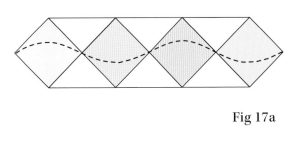

Fig 17a

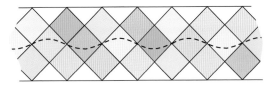

Fig 17b

Patterns

Fig 1a
Pattern (left side) – shown half size, so enlarge by 200% on a photocopier
Blue dashed lines indicates centre line of butterfly and centre point of the motif
Red angled lines indicate placement for edges of the background square
R = reversed

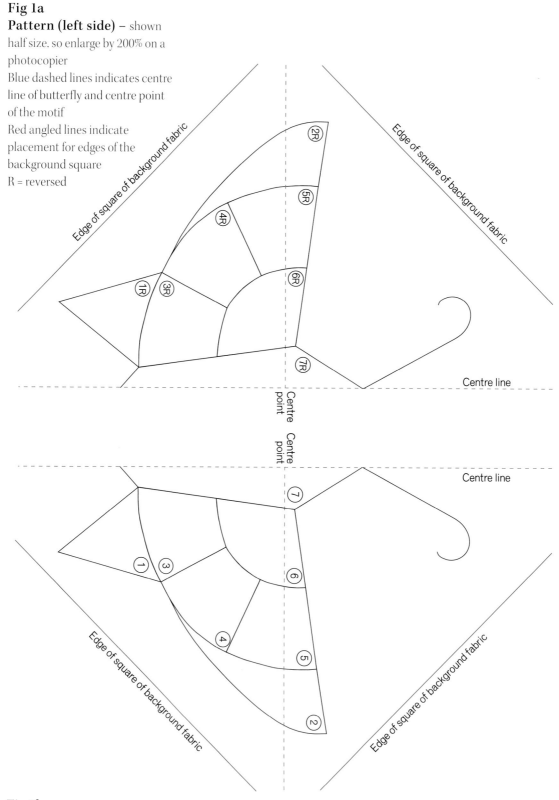

Fig 1b
Pattern (right side) – shown half size, so enlarge by 200% on a photocopier

Fig 2
Pattern Pieces (reversed design) – shown
half size, so enlarge by 200% on a photocopier
Dashed lines indicate where one appliqué piece fits
under another
Arrows indicate fabric grain

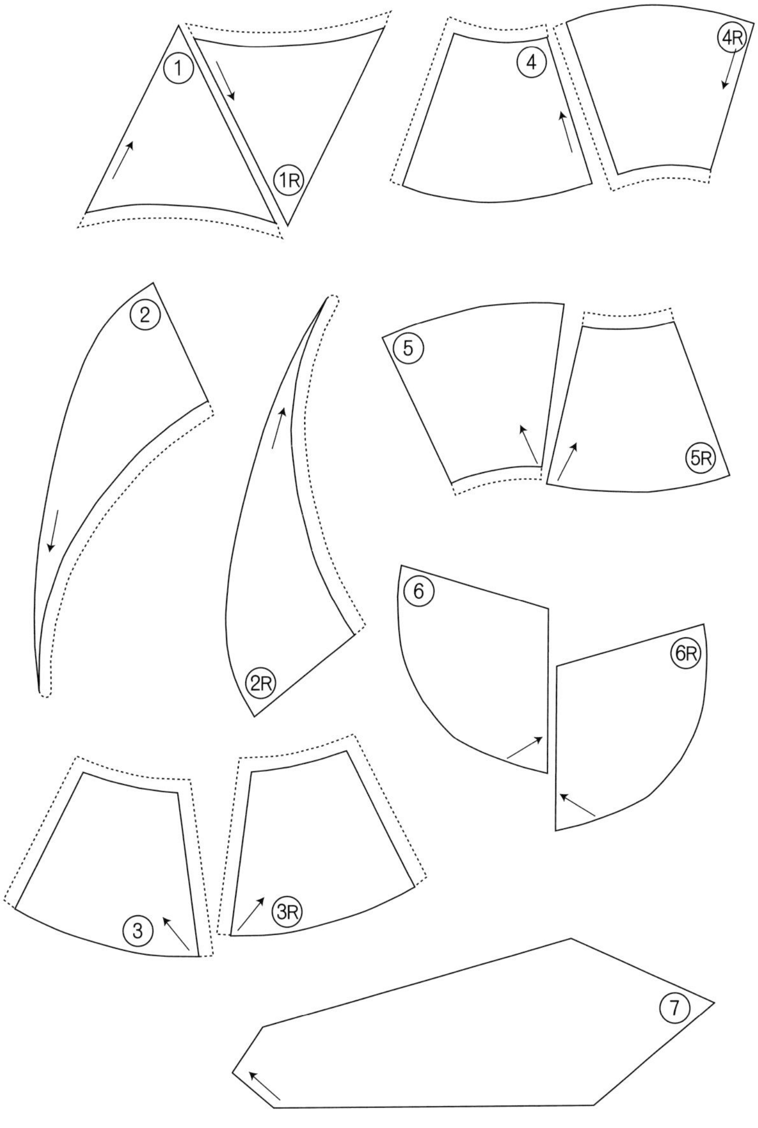

Butterfly Runner and Napkins

Butterflies are always popular as a design, whether in graphics, interior décor or quilts. Having made my Butterfly Quilt I had requests for a smaller design that would be suitable for smaller scale projects like baby quilts, cushions and this table runner. I could have just reduced the original design on a photocopier to an appropriate size, but decided to simplify it to make it less fussy in the smaller size. This new version is shown in Fig 1 at the end of the project instructions. When designing the arrangement of the butterflies on the table runner, I felt that an even smaller version was needed to be placed at the angled ends of the runner and also in the corners of matching napkins. The really small version (Fig 4) I made simpler still, so now you have three sizes and variations in butterfly design which could be used in other projects in the future in addition to the large quilt and the table accessories shown here.

I have also tackled the problem of trying to bind the edges of a quilt that has corners that are not a straightforward 90 degree right angle. Regular binding can be difficult to get looking good, so I have avoided that by adding a final border that will finish just ½in (1.3cm) wide, looking just like binding around the edges of the runner.

Requirements

For the runner:

- Background fabric ¼yd/m, cut as a long strip
- Border fabric ¼yd/m, cut as a long strip
- Backing and binding fabric 1yd/m
- Fabrics for appliqué butterflies – left-overs of border and backing fabric plus two more fabrics, about 12in (30.5cm) square of each
- Fusible web ½yd/m
- Wadding (batting) 50in x 14in (127cm x 35.6cm)
- Threads for the blanket stitch and antennae

For four napkins:

- Four squares of fabric each 13½in (34.3cm) square
- Scraps of the butterfly fabrics to make the appliqué, one on each napkin

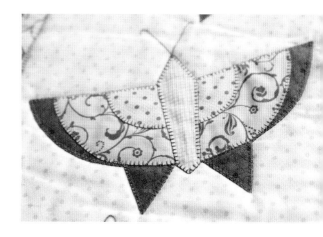

Size of finished table runner:

48in x 12¼in (122cm x 31.1cm)

Size of finished napkin:

12in x 12in (30.5cm x 30.5cm)

TIP

Because this is quite a complex design, I would strongly recommend using either a see-through appliqué pressing sheet or sheets of non-stick parchment baking paper when building up each butterfly (see Tools for the Task: Fusible Web).

Making the Table Runner

1 **Making the butterflies:** The appliqué pieces are stuck in place with a narrow strip of fusible web before edging with blanket stitch, either by hand or by machine. The larger butterfly (Fig 1) uses four different fabrics while the smaller one (Fig 4) uses three. Use the patterns given at the end of the project instructions (enlarging them as described). Six larger butterflies are needed and two smaller ones. Use Fig 1 to choose the fabrics for the larger butterflies. The pieces in the right wing are numbered 1–5, while their opposites in the left wing are numbered 1R–5R (R = reversed: each piece for the right-hand wing is drawn in reversed form for the left-hand wing).

2 When using a fusible web the design must be reversed. Fig 2 gives each reversed shape to make the butterfly design. Place the fusible web smooth side *uppermost* over the nine shapes in Fig 2. Trace each section including any dashed areas. Follow the instructions in Essential Techniques: Using Fusible Web for tracing and cutting out the shapes from the web.

3 Carefully cut out the central area of fusible web from each piece and remove it, leaving only about ⅛in (3mm) inside the drawn line (Fig 3).

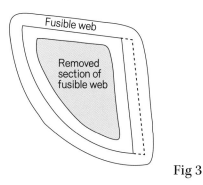

Fig 3

4 Take the four fabrics chosen for the butterfly wings and one for the butterfly body. Place each cut piece of fusible web with the rough side *downwards* on the *wrong* side of each chosen fabric, matching the grain line arrow with the grain or weave of the fabric. Press with an iron to stick the fusible web to the fabric.

5 Now cut accurately along the drawn line through both paper and fabric. Include in the cut-out shape any dashed area.

6 **Building up the design:** To position each piece work on an ironing surface. Trace the design from Fig 1 on to thin paper or tracing paper (or photocopy it). Cut non-stick parchment baking paper a little larger than the finished design in Fig 1 or use a see-through appliqué pressing sheet.

7 If you are using an appliqué pressing sheet, lay it over Fig 1 – you will be able to see the design through the sheet. The baking parchment paper is less transparent but still should allow the design to show through well enough for positioning the pieces on to it. The whole design will be assembled and ironed on to the pressing sheet or parchment paper. Once it is complete, only then will it be peeled away from the plastic or paper and re-positioned and ironed in place on the background fabric. Arrange the cut shapes on the pressing sheet or parchment paper (*not* on the background fabric), right side *up*, glue side *down,* using the drawn butterfly as a guide for positioning.

8 Starting with pieces 1 and 1R (the right wing point and the matching reversed left wing point) remove the paper backing. Position the two shapes right side *up*, glue side *down* in the correct place on the pressing sheet or parchment paper. Iron them on to the sheet or paper to stick them down.

9 Place pieces 2 and 2R into position and iron in place. Position pieces 3 and 4, 3R and 4R, making sure they overlap and fit together with a smooth outline before fixing them with the iron. Finally, add the butterfly body, piece 5, and iron it on to complete the design. Now carefully ease the butterfly away from the pressing sheet or parchment paper.

10 In the same way make five more large butterflies, (a total of six), following steps 8–9.

11 The small butterfly in Fig 4 uses only three fabrics for the wings with one for the body. The reversed shapes are given in Fig 5. Take the four chosen fabrics and follow steps 2–9 to assemble a small butterfly. The numbered pieces are *not* the same (there is no piece 5 – the body is piece 4 for this little version) but the process is very similar. Repeat the process to make a total of two small butterflies. You should now have six large and two small butterflies assembled, ready to position on the background fabric.

12 **Positioning the butterflies:** From your background fabric cut a rectangle 43in x 9in (109.2cm x 22.9cm). If your fabric is only 42in (106.7cm) wide just arrange the butterflies a little closer together and make the finished runner a little shorter.

13 To make the pointed ends, mark the centre of each short end of the fabric and 4½in (11.4cm) down from each corner as shown in Fig 6a. Join up the marks with a drawn line as in Fig 6b and cut along the drawn lines to remove the corners (Fig 6c).

14 Fold the long piece of background in half and crease it to mark the centre. Open it out with right side upwards and position two large butterflies on to it, each with their wing tips ½in (1.3cm) from the centre crease (Fig 7a). Place them so that they are facing straight towards the pointed ends of the fabric, like aircraft on a runway. Press them into place with a hot iron on the background fabric, or you may prefer to pin them into position at this stage and not fix them permanently until all the butterflies have been arranged.

15 Place the two small butterflies centrally at either end of the background strip with their heads 2¼in (5.7cm) from the pointed end of the background strip (Fig 7b). Iron or pin them in position as before.

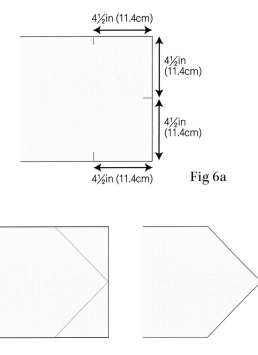

Fig 6a

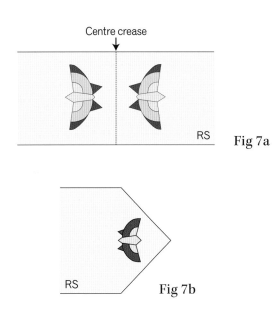

Fig 7a

Fig 7b

Fig 6b   Fig 6c

16 Now arrange the remaining four large butterflies evenly (see photo). A slight angle in the direction of each butterfly makes it look more natural. Once you are happy with your arrangement, press with the iron to fix all the appliqué shapes to the background fabric.

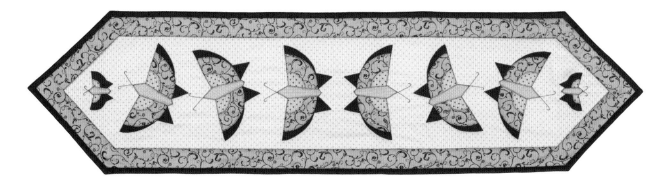

17 Trace the lines of the antennae on to the background fabric with a fine marking pencil.

18 **Stitching the design:** I blanket stitched the design by machine, using normal sewing thread in a contrast colour, but if you wish to stitch it by hand, that will be fine. Use a slightly thicker thread than usual (I used Gütermann silk thread) and a fine sewing needle like a Sharps 9 or 10. Black is often used to outline this type of design, but any choice of colour thread will be fine. See Tools for the Task: Threads and Needles for more information on your choices. For blanket stitching refer to Essential Techniques: Blanket Stitching by Hand or Blanket Stitching by Machine.

19 Stitch the butterflies' antennae by hand, either in backstitch or stem stitch as both make a solid line of stitching. I kept the runner more stable by not cutting away any back layers behind the appliqué at all.

Assembling the Runner

1 From the border fabric cut two strips each measuring 2in x 36in (5.1cm x 91.4cm). Pin and stitch them to either side of the background strip (Fig 8a) – they should be slightly longer than the edges of the runner. Press the seams outwards, away from the background fabric and trim the corners to match the angle of the pointed ends of the runner (Fig 8b).

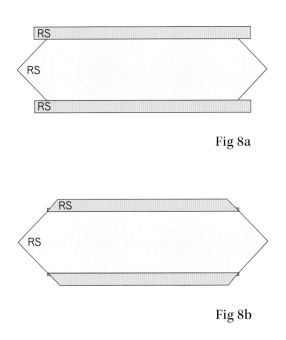

Fig 8a

Fig 8b

2 From the border fabric cut two strips each 2in x 9in (5.1cm x 22.9cm) and two strips each 2in x 10½in (5.1cm x 26.7cm). Take one of the shorter strips and pin and stitch it to one end of the runner (Fig 9a), matching the square corner of the runner with one end of the border strip. Press the seam outwards, away from the runner.

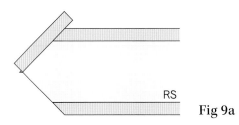

Fig 9a

3 Pin and stitch one of the longer strips to the other raw edge of the runner (Fig 9b), matching the square corner of the runner with one end of the border strip. Press the seam outwards as before. Trim the long ends of the border strips to match the sides of the runner (Fig 9c).

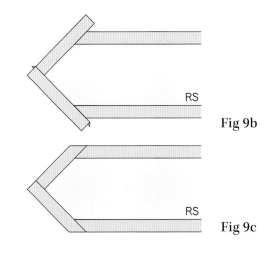

Fig 9b

Fig 9c

4 Repeat this process to pin and stitch the remaining strips of border fabric to the other end of the runner.

5 To add the final narrow binding border, cut from the chosen fabric two strips, each 1in x 37in (2.5cm x 94cm). Follow step 1 above to pin and stitch them to the two long sides of the runner.

6 From the same fabric cut two strips each 1in x 10in (2.5cm x 25.4cm) and two strips each 1in x 11in (2.5cm x 28cm). Repeat the process used before to pin and stitch the four strips to both ends of the runner.

7 From the backing fabric chosen for the runner cut two pieces, each 14in x 25½in (35.6cm x 64.8cm). Stitch them together, leaving a section about 6in (15.2cm) long in the centre unstitched (Fig 10a). Press the seam open, including the unstitched section (Fig 10b).

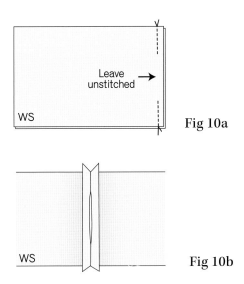

Fig 10a

Fig 10b

8 Trim the backing and the cut piece of wadding (batting) to fit the front of the runner exactly. Layer the three pieces in this order – wadding, then the front of the runner right side *up* and then the backing fabric, right side *down*, matching all the edges exactly. Pin the layers together around the edges.

9 Using the walking foot, stitch a ¼in (6mm) seam around all the edges. Trim the corners a little to reduce the bulk and turn the runner through to its right side through the unstitched section of the backing fabric. Press the edges of the runner and stitch the gap in the backing fabric before quilting the design.

Quilting the Runner

10 I quilted my runner minimally. First, I outlined the butterflies with the same thread that I used for the blanket-stitched edges, machining very closely to the blanket stitch, so it added more strength to the outlines without showing as a separate design. Then I switched to my beloved machine blanket stitch to sew along the inner edge of the wide border strips, using the walking foot so that the stitch acted as quilting through all the layers. Finally, I stitched a machine straight stitch in the seam of the narrow outer border, which completed the illusion of a binding around the outer edge of the piece.

Making the Napkins

1 From the chosen napkin fabric cut four squares each 13½in x 13½in (34.3cm x 34.3cm). Press over a ¼in (6mm) turning to the wrong side of the fabric along all four edges. Fold over once more using the iron to make a ½in (1.3cm) turning on all four sides. Pin or tack (baste) the folded edges in place.

2 Topstitch the seams by machine, using a contrast thread. I also used a decorative stitch to add an extra finish to the edging of the napkins.

3 Follow the instructions in the Table Runner, step 11 to make four small butterflies, one for each napkin. Position one butterfly in a corner of each napkin as shown in the photograph – I placed mine with the butterfly's tail 2in (5.1cm) from the corner of the napkin. Press with a hot iron as usual to fix the butterflies in place on the napkin fabric.

4 Stitch around the raw edges of the butterflies with blanket stitch to match those on the table runner. This is one time when the back of the blanket stitching will be visible, as the napkin is not lined, so the ends of thread will have to be hidden from view. Take all the threads to the back of the work and finish off as neatly as possible. Pull the long threads between the layers of fabric under the butterfly with a needle and cut the ends close to the surface of the fabric.

Patterns

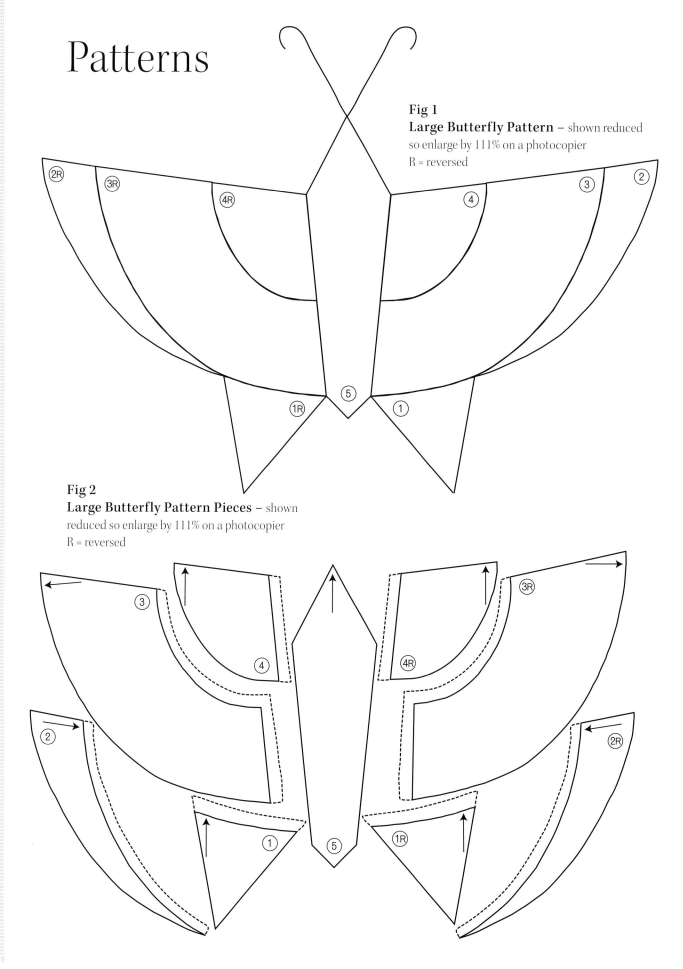

Fig 1
Large Butterfly Pattern – shown reduced
so enlarge by 111% on a photocopier
R = reversed

Fig 2
Large Butterfly Pattern Pieces – shown
reduced so enlarge by 111% on a photocopier
R = reversed

Fig 4
Small Butterfly Pattern – shown reduced
so enlarge by 111% on a photocopier
R = reversed

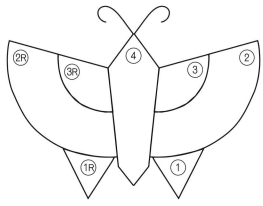

Fig 5
Small Butterfly Pattern Pieces – shown reduced
so enlarge by 111% on a photocopier
R = reversed

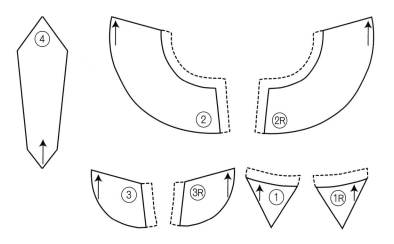

General Techniques

This final section provides general information on finishing your quilt and includes how to add borders, back your quilt and bind the edges. There are also some ideas on quilting.

Bordering a Quilt

Quilts do not always have to have borders, indeed, some look best without any extra border at all. Other quilts are so busy that they just need one or two simple frames around them. It doesn't matter if a fabric has not been used in the quilt as long as it looks as though it belongs. The projects in this book give instructions on adding borders and you will find this general information useful, especially if you want to change or adapt the designs.

A 3in–4in (7.6cm–10.2cm) border for a bed quilt can be cut from 1yd/m of fabric, while 1½yd/m would give a wider border with just one central join on each side. You can get away with several joins in a border strip provided they are placed at regular intervals so that they look planned.

Adding a Framing Border

1 Lay the quilt top on a flat surface and measure its length down the *centre*, not the edge. If you always do this and cut the borders to match the centre measurements there is less danger of the quilt edges spreading and creating wavy borders.

2 Cut two strips of border fabric in the chosen width to match the quilt measurement – these will make the side borders. Pin and stitch each side strip to the quilt, easing in any fullness in the quilt as you pin. Work on a flat surface and match the centres and both ends before pinning the rest. Use ¼in (6mm) seams and once sewn press the seams outwards, away from the quilt (Fig 1).

3 Measure the quilt plus side borders from side to side across the centre. Cut two strips of border fabric in the chosen width to match this measurement. Pin and stitch these to the top and bottom of the quilt, matching centres and both ends (Fig 2). Press the seams outwards, away from the quilt.

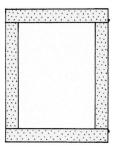
Fig 2

4 If another border is planned, measure the quilt down its centre and repeat the process, sides first and then top and bottom.

Adding a Border with Cornerstones

1 You may prefer to make your border with cornerstones, that is, a square of different fabric in each corner of the border (Fig 3). Measure the quilt across its centre in both directions and cut strips of the border fabric in your chosen width and in lengths to match these measurements. Stitch the side strips to the quilt in the usual way. Press the seams outwards, away from the quilt.

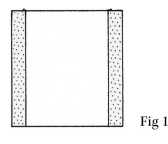
Fig 1

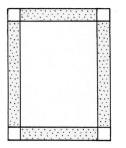
Fig 3

2 Cut four squares of fabric for the cornerstones the same size as the cut width of the border strips. Stitch one of these to either end of both top and bottom border strips (Fig 4). Press the seams towards the long strip. Pin and stitch these border strips to the top and bottom of the quilt, matching seams carefully (Fig 5). Press seams outwards, away from the quilt.

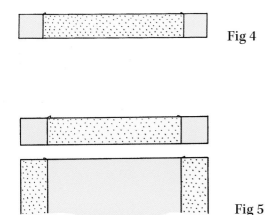

Fig 4

Fig 5

3 If a second border with cornerstones is planned, re-measure the quilt after the first border is added and repeat the process (Fig 6).

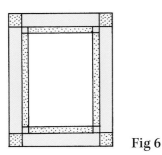

Fig 6

Adding Pieced Borders

Having framed your quilt with one fabric, you may decide it needs a pieced border next. One option is to echo an element of the main quilt design in the pieced border. A pieced border gives the chance to really use up fabric left-overs, even if they have to be supplemented with extra, new fabrics. As long as the colours tone with the quilt, pieces of fabric scrounged from quilter friends to add to your own will fit in surprisingly well.

Backing a Quilt

You can combine several fabrics in a quilt back, which can also create extra interest. If you have a piece of something special that you just cannot bear to cut up, use it as the centre panel of the quilt back and build out from it with strips of other complementary fabrics (Fig 7). Make the piecing as simple as possible since it is more difficult to match exactly the front and back designs if the back is too complex. A series of wide vertical strips in different fabrics can be very pleasing (Fig 8). If the fabric lengths are not enough for this, add horizontal strips at the top and bottom (Fig 9).

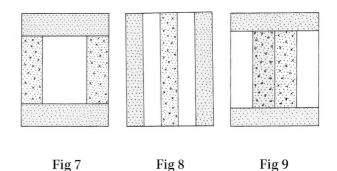

Fig 7   **Fig 8**   **Fig 9**

Should you hanker to combine quilt left-overs in a pieced design for the back, limit this to the centre area and surround it with wide strips or pieces of other fabrics (Fig 10). If the back shifts during quilting and finishes up not quite square against the front, this is far more noticeable when there are narrow border strips around the edges of the quilt back.

Do not agonize that the quilting done from the front will not relate to the piecing on the back. It is surprising how compatible they seem when you turn the quilt over. Just take extra care when putting the layers together to centre both front and back sections as accurately as possible.

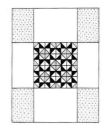

Fig 10

Quilting

I am not concerned here with the various techniques of quilting – there are plenty of books that deal with this. I do suggest, however, that you find a way of quilting the project that gives you satisfaction. The first question is, do you *like* quilting? Do you enjoy quilting by hand or by machine? Remember that you can combine hand and machine quilting. I find tacking (basting) a large quilt very tedious and don't have the space to do it efficiently at home, so will often safety pin the layers thoroughly and begin with a skeleton design of machine quilting using a walking foot to keep everything in place. Then I add more intricate quilting by hand, removing the safety pins as necessary to accommodate a quilting hoop.

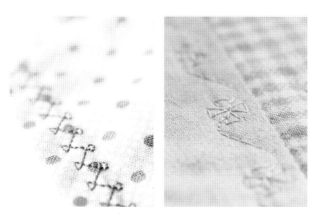

I also encourage my students to explore the embroidery stitches that so many of us have on our machines. It is surprisingly easy to combine one of these with the walking foot to create a line of decorative stitching through all the layers to act as quilting. Choose a simple pattern like a herringbone, avoiding any that make a design with satin stitch as these can get stuck at seam junctions and build up into a lump. Always make a little sample of a top layer, wadding and backing to experiment with before starting on the quilt. Decorative stitches take forever to unpick so make all the mistakes and adjustments on the practice piece. You may find that the width or length of the stitches can be altered. Reducing the stitch width can make a pattern less dominant while increasing the stitch length can stretch the pattern out and make it easier to use as quilting.

Free-machine quilting, when the underneath feed-dogs are dropped and you just doodle with the needle going in any direction that takes your fancy, needs lots of committed practise before trying it on a real quilt.

If you really do not enjoy quilting or just do not have the time, there is always the option of getting the quilt professionally quilted with a long-arm machine. I feel no guilt about not doing everything myself. I love quilting but like most quilters have too many ideas and not enough time to make them all. If you want to use someone else's talents to complete a project, find a professional quilter whose work you admire and enjoy her expertise.

You might feel that some projects will look better without any quilting and prefer to tie the layers together.

Preparing a Quilt Sandwich

A quilt sandwich is the term used for the layers formed from the quilt front, the wadding and the quilt backing. These layers are secured together before quilting begins. Various methods can be used but I suggest that if hand quilting, you tack (baste) the layers together with running stitches ¾in–1in (1.9cm–2.5cm) long, using a long, fine needle. Work from the centre of the quilt outwards in a grid of vertical and horizontal lines about 3in–4in (7.6cm–10.2cm) apart.

If machine quilting, use 1in (2.5cm) safety pins at a distance of 3in–4in (7.6–10.2cm) over the quilt. Tacking (basting) stitches are not suitable when machine quilting as they catch in the feet while stitching. Keep the pins well clear of the areas to be quilted so that they do not get in the way of the machine foot as it stitches.

Marking the Quilting Design

I try to avoid marking a quilt with pencil lines as much as possible. Outline quilting lines, which are usually ¼in (6mm) away from seam lines, can be sewn by eye or by using ¼in (6mm) wide low-tack masking tape. Stick the tape lightly to the surface of the top fabric with one edge against the seam line. Quilt close to the other edge and remove the tape immediately stitching is completed.

Curved designs can be made by placing drinking glasses or plates on the fabric and marking around the edge. You could also use a set of acrylic circles in various sizes and a marking tool called a hera. This is a gem of a tool that I recommend to all quilters. It has an edge rather like a butter knife that makes a sharp crease in fabric when drawn firmly across its surface. It works well against the edge of a ruler to give straight lines for quilting and even around a curved edge. The line can be removed by damping the fabric slightly and letting it dry naturally. If I need to mark with a pencil I use watercolour pencils in a colour that tones with the fabric. This wears away in time and washes out.

Knotting or Tying a Quilt

Tying the quilt layers together with knots is an efficient way of holding everything in place, either instead of quilting or alongside quilting in areas like seam junctions. The slip knot described here is quick and secure.

1 Mark the position of each knot to be made with a glass-headed pin, removing the pins as you make each knot. Knots can be made either on the front of the quilt as part of the design or on the back. For really discreet knotting, work from the back of the quilt using thread that matches the front, changing the thread colour where necessary. Knots need to be a maximum of 3in–4in (7.5cm–10.2cm) apart if they are the only method of holding the layers of the quilt together.

2 To make a knot, use a double thickness of normal sewing thread or thicker embroidery thread if you prefer. Quilting thread is not suitable as it is waxed and is too springy to hold the knot securely. Work from whichever side of the quilt that the knots will be made, and push the needle straight through all quilt layers. Pull the needle through, leaving about 2in (5cm) of thread on the surface of the quilt. Bring the needle straight back up through the quilt about ⅛in– ¼in (3mm–6mm) away from the point where it came through (Fig 11).

3 Hold the 2in (5cm) length of thread straight. Take the needle behind it to the left, then across the front to the right (Fig 12). Bring the needle up through the loop to form a slip knot (Fig 13). Pull the needle until the knot begins to tighten (Fig 14). Pull both ends of the thread to tighten the knot. Trim both threads to about ⅜in (1cm) or leave them longer if you want a more decorative effect.

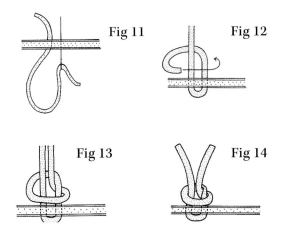

Fig 11

Fig 12

Fig 13

Fig 14

Binding a Quilt

I describe two methods for binding a quilt here; one that uses four strips of binding with squared corners, which is suitable for designs with a horizontal and vertical emphasis such as sashed quilts, and one that uses continuous binding with mitred corners.

Before adding the final binding, check that the quilt lies flat and that the corners are really square. Tacking (basting) with small stitches near to the edge of the quilt will help keep the quilt flat and avoid wavy edges. Trim the wadding (batting) and backing fabric down to a scant ¼in (6mm) beyond the quilt top.

Joining Binding Strips

It is likely that the strips for the binding will have to be joined to make the lengths needed for the quilt. You may even want to add to the overall design with a multi-fabric binding, where many short lengths have been joined. The binding will lie flatter and be easier to handle if the joins are made on the bias, making a 45-degree angle with the long edges of the strip. When stitching the binding to the quilt, use a machine walking foot so all layers are fed through the machine evenly.

1 Cut all strips for the binding 2½in (6.3cm) wide. Trim
the ends of each strip at an angle of 45 degrees as in
Fig 15. To do this, position the 45 degree line on a rotary
ruler along the top of the strip and cut along the ruler's
edge (Fig 16).

2 To join the strips, place two strips as in Fig 17 with
right sides facing. Stitch a ¼in (6mm) seam as
shown. Press the diagonal seam open.

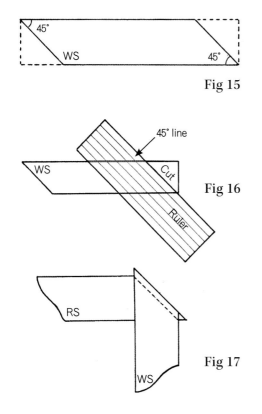

Fig 15

Fig 16

Fig 17

Square-Cornered Binding

1 Cut four strips of fabric for the binding, each 2½in
(6.3cm) wide. The two side strips should measure
the length of the quilt from top to bottom. The two strips
for the top and bottom edges should measure the width
of the quilt from side to side plus 1½in (3.8cm). Shorter
lengths can be joined if you do not have enough fabric.

2 Take each side binding strip and fold it in half, right
side *outwards*, without pressing. Pin a folded strip to
one side of the quilt, matching the edges of the binding
with the edge of the quilt top (Fig 18). Stitch a seam
¼in (6mm) from the edge of the quilt top through all the
layers (Fig 19). Repeat this with the second strip on the
other side of the quilt.

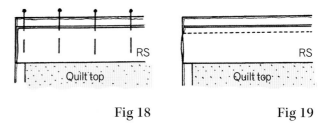

Fig 18   **Fig 19**

3 Now bring the folded edge of the binding over to the
back of the quilt and stitch by hand, just covering
the line of machine stitches (Fig 20).

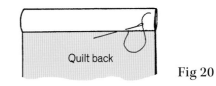

Fig 20

4 Pin and stitch the folded binding to the top and
bottom of the quilt in the same way, leaving about
¾in (1.9cm) of binding extending beyond the quilt at
each end (Fig 21). Trim this back to about ½in (1.3cm)
and fold in over the quilt edge (Fig 22). Finally, fold the
binding over to the back of the quilt and slipstitch in
place (Fig 23). Make sure that the corners are really
square before you stitch them.

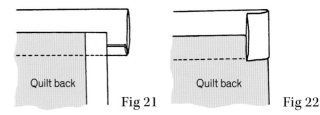

Fig 21   **Fig 22**

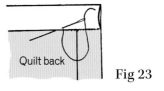

Fig 23

Continuous Binding with Mitred Corners

1 Make a length of binding strip 2½in (6.3cm) wide and
long enough to go right round the quilt, plus about
11in (28cm) to allow for turning corners and overlapping
at the start and finish. Both ends of the binding should
be trimmed on the diagonal.

2   Fold the binding in half lengthwise, right side outwards, and press the entire length. Fold and press a ¼in (6mm) seam to the wrong side of one diagonal end of the length of binding.

3   Starting with this folded end, pin the folded binding strip along one side of the quilt, matching the binding edges with the quilt edge. Do not begin at a corner. Instead, make the start and finish of the binding some way down one side where it will be less obvious (Fig 24). Pin to exactly ¼in (6mm) from the nearest corner of the quilt top. Mark this point on the binding with a dot (Fig 25).

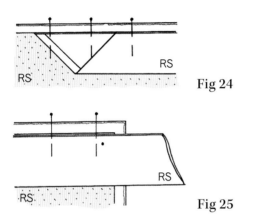

Fig 24

Fig 25

4   Begin stitching 4in–5in (10.2cm–12.7cm) from the start of the pinned binding, using a ¼in (6mm) seam allowance. Finish exactly on the marked dot, backstitching to secure the seam.

5   Remove the quilt from the machine and place it on a flat surface ready for pinning the next side. Fold the binding back at right angles from the stitched side (Fig 26). Now fold the binding down again with the top fold level with the edge of the wadding and backing, and the raw edges level with the edge of the quilt top (Fig 27).

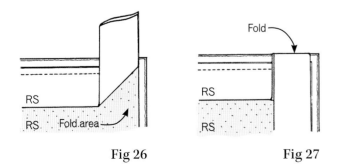

Fig 26   Fig 27

6   Pin the folded layers in place and continue to pin the binding to the side of the quilt until it reaches the next corner. Mark the turning corner ¼in (6mm) from the edge of the quilt top with a dot as before.

7   Stitch the pinned binding with the ¼in (6mm) seam, starting at the edge of the quilt (Fig 28) and continuing to the marked dot. Backstitch to secure the seam at the dot.

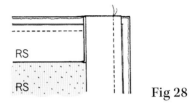

Fig 28

8   Continue to pin and stitch the binding to the quilt, one side at a time, using the method above for turning each corner. On the final side where the binding starts and finishes, slip the finished end of the strip between the layers of the other end of the binding. Trim it so that the folded edge of the beginning section overlaps the end piece by about ½in (1.3cm) (Fig 29). Pin the overlapped sections and stitch.

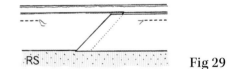

Fig 29

9   Fold the binding over to the quilt back and slipstitch it in place by hand. The front corners will form a mitre, which can be tweaked into place and left unstitched as a diagonal fold (Fig 30). The diagonal overlap where the two ends of binding meet can be left unstitched or be made more secure by hand stitching in matching thread. The corners on the back of the quilt should be arranged into a mitre by folding one side down and then the other. Arrange the fold in the opposite direction to the fold on the front to distribute the layers evenly and make a flat corner.

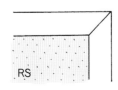

Fig 30

About the Author

Lynne Edwards teaches and demonstrates a wide range of patchwork and quilting techniques, both hand and machine. She has written several textbooks that are considered to be definitive works. Her previous books for David & Charles are: *The Sampler Quilt Book* (1996), *The New Sampler Quilt Book* (2000), *Making Scrap Quilts to Use It Up* (2003), *Stash-Buster Quilts* (2006), *Cathedral Window Quilts* (2008) and *The Essential Sampler Quilt Book* (2010).

In 1992 Lynne was awarded the Jewel Pearce Patterson Scholarship for International Quilt Teachers. This was in recognition of her outstanding qualities as a teacher and included a trip to the Houston Quilt Market and Festival. The award led to invitations to teach as part of the Houston Faculty in 1993 and 1995 and at the Symposium of the Australasian Quilters' Guild in Brisbane in 1993. Since then international teaching trips have included venues in Europe, in Missouri, USA and the National Quilt Show in South Africa. In 2000, teaching commitments included Durban in South Africa and the National Canadian Festival, Canada in 2000. Recent overseas teaching trips include Ireland, France, Spain, New Zealand, Singapore, Dubai, Oman and Kenya.

Lynne's long association with the quilting movement, both locally and nationally, has involved her in the organization of quilt shows – from local village halls to the Quilters' Guild National Exhibitions. She has served on selection committees and is an experienced judge of National Quilt Shows. She was Senior Judge at the South African Quilt Show in 1998, her first experience of judging overseas. In 2000, Lynne was given honorary lifetime membership of the Quilters' Guild of the British Isles, and in 2002 was awarded the Amy Emms Memorial Trophy for services to quilting. In 2008 Lynne was awarded an MBE for her services to arts and crafts.

Acknowledgments

My thanks to the following people. To all the team at David & Charles, who help smooth the path and ease the occasional pain. To my ace editor, Lin Clements, who is always on my side and as keen-eyed and diligent as any author could wish for. I wouldn't do a book without her.

To Gütermann for their support over many years, supplying in particular the silk thread I love to use when blanket stitching, and to Janome for their sewing machines which have made it so easy to master the technique of machine blanket stitching. What a support team – how lucky am I?

Index

TECHNIQUES

Dedication

This book is dedicated to the memory of Alison Maudlin, quilter and excellent teacher, much missed by The Monday 'A' Group in Chelworth. Also to Mary Parrish, a real friend in quilting, who first suggested I might try this technique and so opened up years of true stitching pleasure. To Cheryl Brown, whose determination to get this book accepted knew no bounds. My long association with Cheryl at David & Charles has been a pleasure. To our beloved daughter-in-law Vicky, who is the first in the family to actually want to make quilts too. And finally to all those quilters who have become, like me, totally addicted to this technique. There is no cure, I'm glad to say.

A DAVID & CHARLES BOOK
© F&W Media International, Ltd 2012

David & Charles is an imprint of F&W Media International, Ltd
Brunel House, Forde Close, Newton Abbot, TQ12 4PU, UK

F&W Media International, Ltd is a subsidiary of F+W Media, Inc
10151 Carver Road, Cincinnati OH45242, USA

Text and Designs © Lynne Edwards 2012
Layout and Photography © F&W Media International, Ltd 2012

First published in the UK and USA in 2012

Lynne Edwards has asserted the right to be identified as author of this work in accordance with the Copyright, Designs and Patents Act, 1988.

The author and publisher have made every effort to ensure that all the instructions in the book are accurate and safe, and therefore cannot accept liability for any resulting injury, damage or loss to persons or property, however it may arise.

Names of manufacturers and product ranges are provided for the information of readers, with no intention to infringe copyright or trademarks.

A catalogue record for this book is available from the British Library.

ISBN-13: 978-1-4463-0136-4 Hardback
ISBN-10: 1-4463-0136-2 Hardback

ISBN-13: 978-1-4463-0266-8 Paperback
ISBN-10: 1-4463-0266-0 Paperback

Hardback and paperback editions printed in China by RR Donnelley for: F&W Media International, Ltd
Brunel House, Forde Close, Newton Abbot, TQ12 4PU, UK

10 9 8 7 6 5 4 3 2 1

Acquisitions Editor: Katy Denny
Desk Editor: Jeni Hennah
Project Editor and Diagrams: Linda Clements
Senior Designer: Victoria Marks
Photographers: Lorna Yabsley and Karl Adamson
Senior Production Controller: Kelly Smith

F+W Media publishes high quality books on a wide range of subjects. For more great book ideas visit:
www.rucraft.co.uk